BEYOND THE SHATTERED IMAGE

INSIGHTS INTO AN ORTHODOX
CHRISTIAN ECOLOGICAL WORLDVIEW

John Chryssavgis

2nd Edition

LIGHT & LIFE PUBLISHING
MINNEAPOLIS, MINNESOTA

Light and Life Publishing Company
P.O. Box 26421
Minneapolis, MN 55426-0421

Copyright © 2007 2nd edition
Light & Life Publishing Company
Library of Congress Card No. 98-75639

ISBN 1-880971-42-9

Table of Contents

FOREWORD - i

CHAPTER ONE - 1
The Face of the World

CHAPTER TWO - 16
The Church and the World

CHAPTER THREE - 28
The World as Sacrament

CHAPTER FOUR - 71
Divine Immanence and Divine Transcendence

CHAPTER FIVE - 90
The Sacredness of Creation

CHAPTER SIX - 101
The Desert is Alive

CHAPTER SEVEN - 120
The World of the Icon

CHAPTER EIGHT - 141
Sophia - the Wisdom of God

CHAPTER NINE - 165
The Privilege of Despair

EPILOGUE - 177
Discerning the Face of God

Foreword

Life, in all its myriad forms, from the simplest cell to the most complex organism, the person, seeks fulfillment in community. The very thrust of life, its *telos*, is towards community.

All creatures stand on common ground which is to say their very existence is interrelational. So taught Howard Thurman (1900-1982), the African-American minister, poet, mystic, and ecumenist who had a profound understanding of the community of all being. As a child, Thurman had an experience that moved him to spend his life preaching by word and deed that all people stand on common ground with each other, with animals, with all of creation:

As a boy in Florida, I walked along the beach of the Atlantic in the quiet stillness that can only be completely felt when the murmur of the ocean is stilled and the tides move stealthily along the shore. I held my breath against the night and watched the stars etch their brightness on the face of the darkened canopy of the heavens. I had the sense that all things, the sand, the sea, the stars, the night, and I were one lung through which all of life breathed. Not only was I aware of a vast rhythm enveloping all, but I was a part of it and it was a part of me.

Raised in the tradition of African-American Christian spirituality, Thurman as an adult discovered others from very different traditions, places, and times, whose experiences of the common ground of all being resonated with his: the late medieval Rhineland mystic, Meister Eckhart; Saint Francis of Assisi, who spoke to animals and called the sun brother and the moon sister, the Indian poet Tagore; and the South African writer Olive Schreiner, all kindred souls in their experience of and witness to the community of life.

Reading this marvellous and important book by John Chryssavgis made me think of Thurman and of the many voices down through the ages who have insistently reminded us that we exist in relationship to all the world. To the extent that we forget, neglect, or violate the community which grounds us, we frustrate our very selves and efface the image of God within. This book reveals to us the rich tradition within Eastern Christianity that has consistently taught the sacredness of the world and the interrelatedness of human persons with all of life. The radically communitarian vision of Orthodoxy becomes startlingly clear in the patristic teaching that links the salvation of mankind with the salvation of the world. In this view the salvation of the person is integrally connected with the salvation of the world. Again and again, the Orthodox tradition instructs us to feel compassion for the whole universe and every living creature. This salutary and bracing teaching opens up a new depth to our understanding of the community of all being by insisting that the source of our interrelatedness is ultimately and mysteriously the community of Divine Persons in the Trinity. The Orthodox tradition that Fr. Chryssavgis so clearly and cogently articulates in the text you are about to begin speaks a prophetic word that our world desperately needs to hear and to heed.

Henry W . Putnam
Professor of Religion

Albert Raboteau
Princeton University

Reviews of the first edition of
Beyond the Shattered Image (1999)

One of the best-kept secrets of the ecumenical movement has been the earth-honoring ecological riches of the Orthodox traditions of theology, spirituality and liturgy... John Chryssavgis offers a taste, and more, in this book. It is a remarkable offering of retrieval, drawing widely from ancient and ongoing traditions and presenting them in highly accessible ways. I use the volume as a teaching text, with much success... The writing is elegant and economic at the same time, and the range impressive... What Chryssavgis has achieved in such brief compass is what now stands as a task for representatives of Christianity's other deep traditions; namely, to tap those traditions for their earth-honoring potential where that exists, and to be a part of their conversion to earth, as dynamic, living traditions, where that does not.
Professor Larry Rassmussen, in Worldviews *(UK)*

John Chryssavgis aims to present the full ecological significance of the Orthodox Christian worldview in its deepest, widest and highest sense. It is a tribute to the maturity and clarity of the author's thought that he is able to accomplish this task in a slim volume of fewer than two hundred pages, and to present an essentially Eastern Orthodox perspective in such an attractive, irenic and winsome way that it should appeal across the denominational board... "All creation," says Chryssavgis, "is a palpable mystery, an immense incarnation of cosmic proportions." He writes with authority and passion, clarity and felicity of expression... Every pastor, every Christian in every denomination, let alone every member of the Orthodox Church who seeks to be faithful to the Church's vocation "for the life of the world," should read this book.
Dr. Vincent Rossi, in Sourozh *(UK)*

The incarnational prospects of creation have not been entirely overlooked by Orthodox Christian writers in the past, having been explored to a limited extent in books by Phillip Sherrard and Metropolitan Paulos Mar Gregorios, in several conferences sponsored by the Ecumenical Patriarchate, and in a sourcebook published by Syndesmos. But Beyond the Shattered Image by John Chryssavgis is the first comprehensive attempt in English to bring to bear the richness of Orthodox thought and spirituality on current environmental issues.
Professor Bruce Foltz, President of the International Association for Environmental Philosophy and author of Inhabiting the Earth *(USA)*

Here is served a profoundly convincing Christianity that is gripping and self-authenticating, a theology fit for the millennium! Beyond the Shattered Image is thrilling, enchanting and irresistible! It will change the life of ordinary Christians and satisfy our yearning for wholeness and completeness in a world where God is mystically present and deeply immanent.
John Perkins, author of The Forbidden Self *(USA)*

In this book, John Chryssavgis has written a wonderful piece of work, glowing and translucent, on ecological theology. In reading it, I wondered if I had not opened one of those rare books that will become a contemporary theological classic. Chryssavgis writes with a light, but sure touch. His knowledge of the Greek fathers is impressive. His delight especially in the Desert fathers gives this book a distinctive insight into the life-embracing asceticism of the desert. This book has behind it ten years of meditation and reflection. It has not come into print until it has been honed and polished with gentle clarity and decisive conviction for the restoration of the shattered image of a marred creation. Chryssavgis has done this before in his work on desert spirituality within the Australian context. Here he is thinking globally about the dangers in which creation lives. Reading this book was an exhilarating, but also humbling experience since one was reading a master of the spiritual life, who has a lovely, mischievous sense of humor... The book has the power to draw one in to see the world and its life in God in a fresh and deeply renewing way.
Rev. Dr. Graeme Ferguson, in Colloquium *(Australia)*

CHAPTER ONE

Introduction

The Face of the World

CONSERVATION AND CONVERSION

In recent years, issues such as climate change, flora and fauna extinction, soil erosion and forest clearance, noise and air pollution have been brought vitally to the fore. With the emphasis in the twentieth century on the individual and the individual's rights, who would have predicted that the rape of nature may become more important than, and even equivalent to, fear for our own survival? No matter how carefully modern man has tried to foster material prosperity and self-sufficiency, it is clear today that certain "cracks" have appeared on the face of the earth. And despite actions in the past that sought to contain or constrain the world, we now face a global problem which affects everyone, regardless of geographical location and social class. Nature, we know, waits like a raged animal in a cage, and it is only a matter of time for it to take revenge. The rupture has already been initiated by us; ecological justice will follow suit, sooner or later, with mathematical precision.

Green perspectives, political lobbies, philosophical attitudes, theology (usually a last resort), all endeavor to grapple with the problem. Yet we seem, so often, to be dealing only with the symptoms, rather than with their causes. People are increasingly showing a commitment to, but seem unconvinced to convert to, a lifestyle that might be the answer to the ecological problem, a problem which threatens the existence (and not simply the well-being) of humanity, as well as the very heart of creation. However, before we can effectively deal with the ecological problem–and our aim surely is to do something, and so to practice what *conservatives* and *preservatives* have faithfully claimed but fatefully failed to do–we must first change both our self-image and our world-view. And *the creation waits with eager longing for this revelation of the children of God* (Rom. 8:19).

The three sections of this book aim precisely at this: that the world both within and without needs to be reconsidered in terms of sacrament. The first few chapters examine the sacredness of the world in terms of its interrelation and interconnection with God. The second section expounds the fundamental principles of the Early Church, particularly as these are reflected in the ascetic tradition of the Christian East. And the final chapters explore some theological and spiritual dimensions of an Orthodox view of the environment.

The purpose is not to belittle individual or collective efforts in restoring a balance in the eco-system. Rather, the urgent intention is to question the way in which we appreciate and interpret the world around us and inside us. And we must admit certain assumptions and presumptions behind the word "environment"; there is, here, an entire world of presupposition and preconception. We humans tend to present and promote the world as an objective reality to be examined, experimented and exploited, rather than as a sacred presence to be loved, transformed and venerated. We tend to overlook the dignity that is proper to the world, and the grace with which it is endowed.

We appreciate that the world should not be regarded as a mere necessity. We admit that we need to live in modest harmony with nature, and not in audacious supremacy over it. We may even accept that the world must be respected as something created in love by a Creator calling everyone and everything into an intimate relationship. But in trying to express or expose the environmental crisis, we are inexorably trapped within our individual desires and our need for self-preservation. People may, for instance, consider the human person as being exclusively apart from and above the rest of creation (a gross form of anthropocentrism), or else they may prefer to contain the human person to a part of and within creation (a more subtle kind of anthropocentrism). The perspective, though, remains that of subjecting the world to our own selfish concerns. The human being is persistently seen as the center of what surrounds humanity–with tragic results. The awareness of the cosmic problem is due primarily to the threat that it poses to our own cozy life. This is why the message for environmental awareness has, at least in the past, been based on individual fear, even though fear is a proven inhibitor and not a good motivator. With all the alarming data that is available about the issues, the coherence of the world is rapidly being lost. The problem, then, becomes one of failing to relate properly towards the cosmos. This failure at relating, in turn, harms both parties in the relationship–not only is it we who suffer, but there is total disharmony and disruption.

ECOLOGY AND THE CHURCH

To a large extent, the Christian Church has also opted for the individualistic world-view[1]. Proof of this, is that:

the 1.5 billion followers of Jesus, 'who had no place to lay his head', now control two thirds of the earth's resources and, on average, are three times better off than their non–Christian neighbors. [Indeed,] ...the life-style and consumption patterns of many people in First World countries are way beyond what the earth can support.[2]

Ironically, it is in those very countries and among those *followers of Jesus* that our *deep ecology* thinking is taking place; similarly, it seems to be the same Christians who condemn oppressive or racist systems, and yet condone racial, religious and especially economic disparity in their own society. Yet it is a theology of the created world, particularly as seen in the Orthodox tradition, which I feel holds out the most hope for an endangered environment. However, this book is not meant as an apologetic defense of church life and practice, but simply an endeavor to articulate some personal insights into this theology.

In our world, there has undoubtedly occurred an unfortunate shift in emphasis: from God to man, from heaven to earth, from liturgical symbolism to mathematical analysis. However, the distinct accent in the Orthodox tradition has always been on the theme of cosmic transfiguration, especially evident in the liturgical texts for Theophany, the feast of Christ's Baptism on the sixth of January. There, as the hymns proclaim, *the nature of the waters is sanctified... the earth is blessed... the heaven is enlightened.* And the prayer of the Great Blessing of the Waters that is read on the day concludes:

So that by the elements of creation, and by the angels, and by human beings, by things visible and invisible, God's most holy name is glorified.

COSMIC LITURGY

The Orthodox Church has retained a more "eucharistic" –and more balanced–view, by proclaiming a world imbued by God and a God involved in the world. Orthodox liturgy offers concrete–"incarnate," if you will–answers to the ultimate questions about salvation from corruptibility and death. Our "original sin" lies in turning from God, manifested in the refusal to view life, and the life of the world, as a matter of interpersonal communication and as a sacrament of communion with the divinity.[3] God is the Lord of the dance of creation, which is a voluntary overflow of divine gratuitousness and grace. A seventh-century writer, Maximus Confessor, describes the divine act of the Incarnation as a re-creation in which:

God is emptied and descends without change to the last extremities of nature.[4]

In a sense, the only duty of humanity is to recognize and, through doxology, to respond to the reality that the human person is–before and beyond any social or individual being, a political or rational animal–a liturgical celebrant of this innate joy in the world. This liturgical dimension of joyful praise in creation is a gift to the world, and does not depend on our environmental efforts or awareness. Augustine long ago recognized this reality:

Through the mouth of the good, all the lands are making a joyful noise to the Lord... No words are needed to make this joy heard... overflowing with joy... above the level of discourse.[5]

Unless we entertain and joyfully enter into this interdependence of all persons and all things in what the same Maximus calls the *cosmic liturgy*,[6] we cannot hope to resolve issues of economy and ecology. We should respond to nature with the same delicacy, sensitivity, and tenderness with which we respond to a person in a relationship. And our failure to do so is the ultimate source of pollution, a consequence of our inability to relate caringly towards the created world.

The way in which we behave towards creation also reflects the objective manner in which we relate to the poor. The term *eco-justice*[7] was coined because all ecological activities–just as all economic programs, and even all theological attitudes (cf. Matt. 25:31f.)–are ultimately measured and judged by their effect upon the poor.

COSMIC IMAGE

The interdependence between ourselves and our world is wonderfully portrayed by a contemporary American writer, Wendell Berry, who touches in a prophetic and healing manner on the deeper implications of our global crisis:

The earth is what we all have in common, that is what we are made of and what we live from, and we therefore cannot damage it without damaging those with whom we share it. But I believe it goes further and deeper than that. There is an uncanny resemblance between our behavior toward each other and our behavior toward the earth. Between our relation to our own sexuality and our relation to the reproductivity of the earth, for instance, the resemblance is plain and strong and apparently inescapable. By some connection that we do not recognize, the willingness to exploit one becomes the willingness to exploit the other. The conditions and the means of exploitation are likewise similar.[8]

Not only are we members one of another (cf. Eph. 5:19), but, to carry Berry's image still further and make an identity of the interdependence, there is an *uncanny resemblance* between our very body and the earth. If the earth is our very flesh, it becomes inseparable from our story, our destiny, and our God. And *no one ever hates one's own flesh* (Eph. 5:29). This attitude echoes the thought of Origen of Alexandria (c. 185-254), according to whom:

The world is like our bodies. It, too, is formed of many limbs and directed by a single soul. Yes, the world is an immense being directed by the power and the word of God, who is, so to say, its soul.[9]

However we may endeavor to disguise our autonomous regard for created matter as a service to humanity and to its progress, we ultimately need to unmask the illusion and to become aware that our individual destiny and purpose are profoundly identified with that of our world, just as we are all susceptible to each other's influence. There is no autonomy, just a distinction between a sense of responsibility and a lack thereof.

In order to know how our world and humanity are interconnected, and together intimately connected with God, we must be able to see all things in God and God in all things. This is the fundamental difference between the *secular* world-view and the *sacred* vision:

The person with a secular mentality feels himself to be the center of the universe. Yet he is likely to suffer from a sense of meaninglessness and insignificance because he knows he's but one human among five billion others–all feeling themselves to be the center of things–scratching out an existence on the surface of a medium-sized planet circling a small star among countless galaxies. The person with a sacred mentality, on the other hand, does not feel herself to be the center of the universe. She considers the Center to be elsewhere and other. Yet she is unlikely to feel lost or insignificant precisely because she draws her significance and meaning from relationship, her connection, with that Center, that Other. [10]

For St. Paul, the difference lies in the face of Christ. He describes Christ as *the image of the invisible God,* and says that:

all things were created through him and for him. He is
before all things, and in him all things hold together.
(Col. 1:15-20, esp. 16-17).

COSMIC VISION

Paul's words are echoed in the monastic literature of the
seventh century by Isaac the Syrian:

What is a merciful heart? It is a heart which is burning
with love for the whole of creation: for humans, for birds,
for beasts, for demons–for all God's creatures.[11]

The tradition is age–old and universal, transcending
time, culture, and disciplines. Hence, in Dostoevsky's
The Brothers Karamazov, the exhortation of Fr. Zossima
is to:

love all God's creation, the whole of it and every grain of
sand. Love every leaf, every ray of God's light. Love the
animals, love the plants, love everything. If you love
everything, you will perceive the divine mystery in
things.[12]

At the end of his life, Zossima reeked of an all-
embracing love, that included his flesh, his humanity,
and the whole world. Such a love for creation smashes
the self-centered, secular world-view and gives us a
sense of enlarged existence. In this way we gain access
to other dimensions of life and are empowered to move
beyond our own lives, to see others and the world around
as part of us and as distinct from us. For we constitute a
part of creation and should never be considered apart

from it, much less so set ourselves up over or against it.
The vision and boundaries of the world are far broader
than the limited space and life of any human being. The
kaleidoscope of creation reveals a variegated splendor of
perception and a rich diversity of beauty, which reflects
the dignity of God. The variety provides a glimpse into
the grandeur of God:

Study the enormous number of different kinds of birds,
the variety of their shapes and colors... It gives me joy to
speak of these things because they unfold to us the
greatness of God.[13]

Thus we understand that we can never exhaust the
essence of even the smallest flower. For when we look at
a flower, we perceive not its intrinsic nature but a
reflection in the flower of the intrinsic nature of our own
consciousness in relation to this flower. Similarly, a bee
only perceives the nectar of the flower; a snake perceives
the same flower as an infrared object; a bat perceives the
flower as an echo of ultrasound. Therefore, the essential
reality of the flower always remains *unobjectifiable,*
beyond our narrow interest and individual indulgence.
Centuries ago, theologians of Cappadocia such as Basil
the Great (d. 379) were aware that the essence of the least
flower and the slightest blade of grass evades human
knowledge:

We cannot understand the nature of these things. Much
less are we likely to be able to understand the nature
of the first Being, the unique Being who is the fullness
of everything.[14]

Such is the breadth and depth of the Orthodox cosmic vision, one that is always larger than that of any one individual. I may be the center of this vision or *theophany*, but I become aware that I am also but a detail of the world. Indeed the world ceases to be something that I observe objectively and becomes something of which I am a part personally and actively. No longer then do I feel as a stranger, i.e. threatened and threatening, but as a friend in and of the world, i.e. caring and loving. How sadly Christians have misinterpreted the words of Christ that we are *in the world* but *not of the world* (cf. John 17:14 and 16). The two verses from John's Gospel should not be detached, still less are they to be divorced, from the middle verse which is a clarification of Christ's prayer:

I am not asking you to take them out of the world, but I ask you to protect them from evil. (v. 15).

Whenever we fail to seek the cosmic vision, we narrow life to ourselves, our concerns and our desires, and neglect the vocation to which we are called to transform the creation of God. Just as whenever we reduce religious life to ourselves, our concerns and our desires, we forget the calling of the Church to implore God–always and everywhere–for the renewal of the whole polluted cosmos. For the Church is a unique symbol. And I use the term symbol not as a way of perceiving reality, but as a profound way of realizing and *reconciling* (the literal translation of the Greek *symbolon* is bringing together) two distinct, though not unrelated realities: divinity and creation, God and world. The Church brings to God the world, for the life of which

God gave his only Son; and the Church also brings God to the world, which God so loved (John 3:16). This reconciliation is the essential function of the Church. The direct opposite of the symbolical is the diabolical world-view. And the diabolical (Greek: *dia-bolos* meaning the one who disperses) heresy of the ecological crisis is the exclusion of the reality of the kingdom of heaven, as well as the dispelling of the intuition that everything is a unique manifestation of that kingdom.

THE SHATTERED IMAGE

An image without any bearing on reality is a meaningless dream; reality without the insight of an image is a senseless drudgery. Heaven and earth are full of God's glory, the world is a burning bush of divine energy, drenched with divine presence. This is the way we received it from our Creator. It remains simply for us to recognize the image for what it is. Creation itself has understood, long before any human anxiety, the need to restore this reality:

From the beginning till now the entire creation, as we know, has been groaning in pain (Rom. 8:22).

Restoring the reality is less a matter of *deconstruction* or *reconstruction* of any philosophical ideologies, as an urgent question of reorientation towards traditional ways of thinking and of rediscovery of ab-original spirituality and mythology. An image, even if shattered, combined with a realistic task can truly change this world, for there is a beauty beyond the shattered image, an *ancient beauty that requires reconstruction* and transformation.[15]

Such is the two-fold purpose of this book: something will have been achieved, if the reader is reminded of the breadth and depth of Orthodox theology (the Scriptures and the Christian classics) and practice (the desert tradition and the liturgy). We need urgently to heal our relationship with the world, and to establish a proper attitude within the order of things. This book is a small contribution to that process–which has been maturing over the last decade–of rethinking and revision, of education and information, of illumination and the awakening of conscience.

There is, however, one important parenthetical remark that must be made from the outset. The *shattered image* is not a problem only of Western Christianity or of Western civilization as such. No single era or culture may be held entirely responsible for contemporary disastrous developments.

It is naive to suppose that Orthodoxy automatically has the key to the answers where others have failed. Certainly Western civilization represents a particular world-view and attitude, but it is pointless to explain the contemporary ecological crisis in terms of a deviation on the part of Western philosophy and theology. So much fine literature has described this crisis as a process which began in the late middle ages, grew in the Reformation and Counter-Reformation, and produced modern enlightenment and technology. Instead, it is essential that everyone–whether of *Western* or *Eastern* origin–faces the godless anthropocentrism that colors our world.

While technology may inspire humanity with a dangerous inclination toward autonomy and self-destruction, one must never forget that the supreme goal of humankind is forever to progress in the sight of the Creator within a continually renewed creation. Therefore, today's immense technical progress ultimately renders humanity more responsible. Consequently, the Church's relationship with and responsibility towards the world, obliges it to exercise a prophetic criticism within highly technological and rapidly changing cultures.

There can be no fixed formula, no definitive solution. Nonetheless, defensive or apologetic attitudes should be abandoned. We must enter into a radical, though responsible criticism of our civilization and of the fundamental presuppositions of life in our world. Clearly it is presumptuous, not to say audacious, to suppose that the Orthodox world-view undeniably presents the *essence* of Christianity–that would once have been termed *the sin of pride*–but it is important for Orthodoxy to rethink its vocation and contribution at the present time. Certainly with regard to creation, Orthodoxy has preserved an unequaled dynamism and unqualified optimism; it has also reserved an unprecedented affirmation of every particle of creation.

It is a paradox that Orthodox spirituality has in the past often been identified as a mystical–in the sense of other-worldly, almost un-worldly–attitude. Yet in its most powerful criticism of the shattered image of our world, Orthodox theology emphasizes precisely the significance of creation as the incarnation of God in the widest and deepest sense. One needs, however, to learn how to discover the penetrating insights offered by the Orthodox world-view. Consequently, the pages that follow seek not so much to impose a particular or peculiar vision, but to awaken a presence, to reveal an image beyond the shattered world around us:

The fact is that God is at work in the world, the same God who infuses into creation the power needed for it to continue stable throughout all time... Through the things that are seen let us be led toward the things that are not seen. To do this there is no need to travel far. Only faith is required, because only through faith can we behold him.[16]

We have progressed to the point where we know better than to treat people like things. It is now time that we learn no longer to treat even things like things, although this practice can only come from an altered perspective and a changed heart. As St John of Kronstadt (1829-1908) notes, we have come to the state where:

...we see flesh and matter in everything, and nowhere, nor at any time, is God before our eyes.[17]

Yet we do not need to travel far to discern the divine image. The dynamic presence of Christ's countenance is a reality perceived through the eyes of faith. This is the conviction of the Orthodox tradition of spirituality. The words from the Psalms are today more relevant perhaps than ever:

I discerned before me [the face of] my Lord in everything (Psalm 16:8). For, *all things look to [His] face...which renews the face of the ground* (Psalm 104:27-30).

CHAPTER TWO

The Church and the World

Religious thought and practice during the middle ages were influenced by the sharp division that the Church made between grace (as divine and uncreated) and nature (as material and created). As a result, people could not overcome the dichotomy, or otherwise failed to distinguish at all, between the sacred and profane, between things divine and things temporal. This manner of thinking prevails to the present day, where it is reflected in people's lack of confidence in the established Church, as well as in their anti-*theism* or anti-*clericalism.* There is need of a restored theological vision–one that is far less separatist, self-sufficient and condemnative toward the world. The Church must learn again to affirm, indeed to assume the world, just as Christians claim that *the Word assumed the [world's] flesh* (John 1:16). People need once more to affirm the breadth of the Church and to discern the beauty of the world. It will, therefore, be helpful briefly to define the key terms to be discussed in this chapter.

THE NOTION OF "WORLD"

There is undoubtedly great diversity in the way people perceive the world and nature. For instance, the world may be considered by some to include everything outside the Church. For the Orthodox tradition, this attitude is clearly inappropriate because the Church is nothing less than the entire world transfigured, the universe ordered, nature rendered into *cosmos*–a term that literally means *beauty*. Indeed, *cosmos* is in fact the only Greek term for the world.

In the minds of others, however, the world may designate the enormous possibilities promised, and even presented, by technology and scientific progress. Both are seen as transforming nature into civilization through human intelligence and with the assistance of material nature and machines. The naive optimism of such a view surely runs the risk of losing sight of the central significance of Gethsemane and Golgotha, of a land of tears and pain and death. *For God so loved the world that he gave his only Son* (John 3:16). Indeed this love-to-the-point-of-death (cf. Phil. 2:8), which constitutes a characteristic feature of the Orthodox understanding of creation, seems to be at the opposite end of Western thought. Instead of dwelling upon individual predestination, Eastern Church Fathers lay great emphasis upon the final cosmic transfiguration. In Western circles, under Augustinian influence, there is a tendency to distort salvation into that which is offered exclusively to a few worthy souls. Orthodox thought tends towards the conviction that, in the end, everyone and everything will be filled with the light of the God who is love (cf. I John 4:8). God in *Christ will become all in all* (Col. 3:11).

Similarly, any discussion of Church and world should not opt for an easy pantheism according to which the world is simplistically and superficially (in this regard, theological manuals of old introduce the term *supernaturally)* equated with the sacred. To be balanced, a Christian understanding of the world must safeguard a biblical duality: for on the one hand the continuity, and on the other hand the discontinuity between Creator and creation need to be underlined. The line of demarcation between God and world is clearly, although not always so sharply, drawn in the Hebrew Scriptures. Therefore, while the Bible accepts the creation of the world by God out of nothing *(ex nihilo),* at the same time it is quick to affirm the creation of humanity *in the image and likeness of God.* (Gen.1:26).[1] Furthermore, the Greek term for Church, *ek-klesia*, implies a *calling out* from the world in order to fulfill the true vocation of the whole world–namely to realize its dynamic relationship with God, to interpret the horizontal and historical in terms of the vertical and eternal. And so again it is the distinction as well as the identity of Church and world that are affirmed.

This means that the Church cannot properly exercise its function unless it cares for every person, for every bird, for every tree, and for every stone in the world. Likewise the Church can never be exhausted in or reduced to sociological analyses, ecological projects, and economic programs. The breadth of the Church's vision lies in the cup of Communion. It has been said that *one is what one eats* (L. Feuerbach). Thus, only with the living body and blood of Jesus Christ as the central plate of life's banquet is one able to catch a glimpse of reality and of what really matters in this world.[2] The dimension of liturgy will be examined later. Here, it is sufficient to underline that a proper evaluation of the world inevitably operates within the framework of the following fundamental dialectic: the goal is always conversion from autonomy to dependence on God, from independence to ecclesial communion, from anthropocentrism to theocentrism. The movement of the world expects the moment of repentance from self-sufficiency to love. Such a conversion of life-style and rhythm is the underlying principle of the chapters in this book.

THE NOTION OF "CHURCH"

At this point, it is important to outline briefly the notion of Church in the Orthodox tradition. What follows is by no means a systematic approach to the question, but an outline in the specific context of our subject matter.

No one can deny that the Roman Catholic Church is a powerful organization and institution, nor can one ignore the active and vital growth of the Anglican and Protestant Churches. Nonetheless, there appears to be a great difference between what Western Christianity and the Orthodox East understand when referring to the notion of Church. A clarification is surely needed here both for theological and ecumenical purposes. Indeed, relations and discussions among the various Churches have in recent times encouraged a study of ecclesiology in order precisely to shed light upon the numerous divisions in the Christian world and to discern a methodology for reconciliation.

From as early as the third century, but especially from the time of Constantine in the fourth century, the Church gradually began to be seen more in juridical terms. This was the case particularly in the West, owing perhaps to the powerful impact of the Roman imperial and legal spirit. The result over the centuries was a reduction of the Church either to a rigorous monarchical system or to a social and political program. The accent in either case appeared to be more on the external, visible organization and on immediate authority, sometimes combining, or even confusing, the power of this world with that of the next. While not altogether losing sight of the inspirational and sacramental aspect, the Church strongly emphasized its institutional or secular dimension as establishment. This attitude of course is also the result, among other things, of a just and justifiable historical evolution.

Yet in the West, the consequence of this development was that the Church imposed itself on society and family, pronouncing and decreeing, at times correctly and courageously but at others possibly incorrectly and even audaciously, from *above* on ethical and moral issues. The impression of many Eastern Orthodox–among whom, admittedly, the more *outward* missionary, social, monastic, liturgical and theological developments have at certain times and places proved deficient–is that the *symphony* between the divine and human has been forfeited in the West for an emphasis on human realism and worldly activism. If the Church is no longer called to transform humanity and the whole created order, but rather is required to conform to a finite worldly reality, then it ceases to be a promise and becomes a compromise.

THE CHURCH AND THE WORLD

While the Church is in the world and exists for the world (cf. John 6:51), its origin and goal, its alpha and omega, lie beyond the world in the divine initiative. Being the instrument of grace in both divine and earthly aspects, even the Church's institutional side reveals the energy of the Holy Spirit, which is the creative and motivating force of everything and everyone. This Spirit is the Giver of life and of all forms of life: personal, interpersonal, communal, ecclesial, and hierarchical.

The fact that the Church is in the world signifies that God penetrates the whole world. Therefore, Church and world cannot be conceived independently of one another. *In the world* means precisely in total solidarity and communion with the world, implying an organic relationship, and not simply a moral or social one. The communion between Church and world is not dependent on actions of clergy or on systems of theology, but it is conferred through the loving act of creation and confirmed with the loving act of *re-creation*, as the Incarnation has come to be known.

The Church then is the world, as the latter was intended to be. And the world is the Church, as the former is called to become. The danger of overemphasizing the Church as the world transfigured or as some *new creation* (Rev. 21:1) is that we may be led to see only the divine, other-worldly aspect of the Church. Yet the world is entirely present in the Church. In fact, the Church needs to remember to be *down to earth*. Christians are called to be *faithful stewards* and trustworthy caretakers of the mysterious dimensions of the earth (cf. I Cor. 4:1-2). For it is precisely by remaining faithful to the earth that the Church also becomes *new heaven* (Rev. 21:1). The *heavenly* penetrates, but in no way imposes itself upon the *earthly*. This is a basic doctrine of the Christian

Church, namely that the earthly aspect of the Church and the world is not crushed but consecrated, never rejected but always respected. This doctrine alone is able to safeguard the Church from any abuse in authority and from all forms of triumphalism. It also avoids any attempt to secularize the Church, since that too is understood as another severance of the relationship between heaven and earth.

The Greek word for devil *(dia-bolos)* implies, as we have already seen, a rupture: the diabolical temptation at all times in the Church is to succumb either to a form of angelism or else to a form of secularism, to find its grounding either in the *other-worldly* or the *very mundane.* What results is the destruction of the equilibrium of the Church in the world and of the world in the Church, as well as the distortion of the vision of harmony between heaven and earth.

VISION OF HEAVEN ON EARTH

Any discussion about the relationship between Church and world, or about the establishment of *a new heaven and a new earth,* involves a study of Christian anthropology. For it is the person renewed in Christ, that is one who has *died* to this world and then *risen* in the light of the world restored in Christ, that acquires a new vision of the world.

Before there can be any social or environmental ethic, there must first be a personal ethos. It is so easy, which is why it remains a great temptation, to introduce abstract and general plans and programs, while neglecting the personal dimension of the Church and the world. What is meant by *personal* is not the individualism so pervasive in our society but rather the relational aspect of creation. This aspect envisages the human person in relation to God, to other human beings (at once created in the image of God, as well as made from the earth), and to the rest of creation.

The person baptized and clothed in Christ (cf. Gal. 3:27) is essentially no different from any other person in the world (cf. Col. 3:11). What distinguishes the Christian believer, however, is the aim to become a Christic or Christ-centered person. An early document of the Church reveals the way of life of the first Christians:

They are in the world, but their piety is unseen... They inhabit both Greek and barbarian cities, as the case may be, and follow the local customs in dress, diet, and life in general... They obey the particular laws, and transcend these very laws with their own life... They live on earth, but their citizenship is in heaven. [3]

Thus, Christians differ only existentially from others inasmuch as *they have put on the new nature which is renewed in knowledge after the image of its creator* (Col. 3:10), namely *Christ who is all in all* (ibid. v. 11). And the word *knowledge* in the passage just quoted carries more weight than may at first be apparent. For it is one thing to preach and affirm the presence of Christ everywhere, and quite another to recognize and reflect Christ in all places and persons:

From now on, then, we know no one from a human (lit., a fleshly) point of view; even though we once knew Christ from a human point of view, we no longer know him thus. Therefore if any are in Christ, they are a new creation; the old has passed away, behold the new has come. All this is from God, who through Christ reconciled us to himself and gave us the ministry of reconciliation; that is, in Christ, God was reconciling the world to himself (II Cor. 5:16-19).

To be *in Christ* is a personal event and an act of faith, but its call to reconciliation makes it also an act of relationship and an event of reconciliation or community. And as an image of what the world is supposed to be, the community of the Church further becomes a cosmic and universal event.

This becoming anew explains the emphasis in Eastern Orthodoxy on the ascetic and ecclesial dimension of Christianity, which will be explored in the following chapter. It also assists us in making sense of the Orthodox emphasis on reconciliation *(metanoia)* and divinization *(theosis),* that will be discussed in the final section of this book. The entire early Christian tradition and in general Orthodox thought affirm that *the Word of God assumed flesh* (John 1:14) so that the world might be reconciled and deified and the whole of creation might share in the grace of divine nature. Ultimately, God became human and assumed the created world in order that creation might become what it was originally intended to be.

SOLUTION OR SALVATION

In a sense, therefore, Orthodox theology proposes no theoretical solution with regard to the problems of the world. What it offers is an invitation to salvation, namely to healing and transfiguration, to be able to see the same situations in a different light. This does not imply subjectivism, for the particular *difference* and *light* are the result of the grace of the Holy Spirit who renews and restores everything. There is nothing in the world that is not a gift of the Spirit. And the goal of the human person is simply to acquire these gifts wherever they are to be found. A balanced view of both Church and world cannot afford to overlook the person and power of the Holy Spirit. Only from this perspective is creation understood as the work of a God who is love and who acts in love, a God who is Trinity and communion, a God who greatly desires to share this communion with the world (cf. Luke 23:15).

A passage taken from *The Revelations of St. Seraphim of Sarov on the End of the Christian Life*, written toward the beginning of the nineteenth century, illustrates, better than any intellectual exposition, wherein this crucial *difference* of the Holy Spirit lies. In the course of a conversation that took place in a forest one winter morning, Motovilov, a disciple of St. Seraphim and the author of these *Revelations*, is speaking to his elder:

All the same, I don't understand how one can be certain of being in the Spirit of God. How should I be able to recognize for certain this manifestation in myself?

"I've already told you," said Father Seraphim, "that it's very simple. I've talked at length about the state of those who are in the Spirit of God. I've also explained to you how we can recognize this presence in ourselves... What more is necessary, my friend?"

"I must understand better everything that you have said to me."

"My friend, we are both at this moment in the Spirit of God. Why won't you look at me?"

"I can't look at you, Father," I replied. "Your eyes shine like lightning, your face has become more dazzling than the sun, and it hurts my eyes to look at you."

"Don't be afraid," said he. "At this very moment you've become as bright as I have. You are also at present in the fullness of the Spirit of God; otherwise, you wouldn't be able to see me as you do see me." And leaning towards me, he whispered in my ear: "Thank the Lord God for His infinite goodness towards us... How thankful we ought to be to God for this unspeakable gift which He has granted to us both... The grace of God, like a mother full of loving kindness towards her children, has deigned to comfort your afflicted heart, at the intercession of the Mother of God herself... Why then, my friend, do you not look me straight in the face? Look freely and without fear; the Lord is with us."

Encouraged by these words, I looked and was seized by holy fear. Imagine in the middle of the sun, dazzling in the brilliance of its noontide rays, the face of the man who is speaking to you. You can see the movements of his lips, the changing expression of his eyes, you can hear his voice, you can feel his hands holding you by the shoulders, but you can see neither his hands nor his body–nothing except the blaze of light which shines around, lighting up with its brilliance the snow-covered meadow, and the snowflakes which continue to fall unceasingly.

"What do you feel?" asked Father Seraphim."An immeasurable well-being," I replied. "Infinite joy in heart."

Father Seraphim continued: "When the Spirit of God descends on a man, and envelopes him in the fullness of His presence, the soul overflows with unspeakable joy, for the Holy Spirit fills everything He touches with joy... If the first-fruits of future joy have already filled your soul with such sweetness, with such happiness, what shall we say of the joy in the Kingdom of Heaven, which awaits all those who weep here on earth... For the present we must work, and make continued efforts to gain more and more strength to attain the perfect measure of the stature of Christ .... But then this transitory and partial joy which we now feel will be revealed in all its fullness, overwhelming our being with ineffable delights which no one will be able to take from us."[4]

The beauty of the world is indeed *in the eye of the beholder.* Yet the beholder must *be held* in the light and joy of the sacrament of the Kingdom.

CHAPTER THREE

The World as Sacrament

If there is one image that presents itself as unique and fundamental in contemporary religious experience, it is that of the land. This was the sentiment expressed by Fr. Zossima, as we saw in the first chapter. It is also the sacramental ethos of the Orthodox Church. *The earth with all its fullness* (Ps. 23:1 and Deut. 33:16) presents to us an undeniable theological truth, a truth that *springs from the earth* (Ps. 85:11). Indeed, if there exists today a vision able to transcend and transform all national and denominational tensions, it may well be that of our world understood as sacrament. And this is a subject, albeit tentative in nature, that is at last being studied.

Unfortunately we have been conditioned to consider the sacraments in far too narrow and reductionist a manner: a fixed number of sacraments, so that all else assumes a non-sacramental tone; minimal requirements for their validity; or an over-emphasis on the hierarchical structure of the Church and the ritualistic nature of liturgy. We need to recall the sacramental principle, which ultimately demands from us the recognition that nothing in life is profane or unsacred. There is a likeness-in-the-very-difference between that which sanctifies (God) and that which is sanctified (creation), between uncreated and created. *The Divine Liturgy of St. John Chrysostom,* which is celebrated each Sunday in Orthodox churches throughout the world, expresses the conviction about God in relation to the world with these words:

You are the one who offers and is offered, who receives and is distributed, Christ our God, and to you we offer glory.

This chapter explores an understanding of sacrament that includes the world, and begins to formulate a theology of creation in light of our dilemma before and response to the current environmental crisis.

A THEOLOGY OF SACRAMENT

One may debate about sacraments and doctrines which either unite or divide people and churches. However, is it not more important to consider the common ground that we all tread–no pun intended–as the source of our solidarity and as the ultimate sign of the communion that we share? The principle according to which the Church exists for the life of the whole world and not simply to satisfy certain religious needs of particular individuals can hardly be overemphasized. In order to appreciate such a comprehensive view of the Church, one must be prepared to acknowledge the sacredness or sacramentality of the world. But we must also confess that too often the dominant view of the world even, and at times especially by people within the Church, is the mechanistic concept, which arrogantly subjects everything to the individualistic desires and conquests of humanity. But this view is far removed from the iconic dimension, that which envisages the whole of Christ in everything, and from the organismic view which is more sensitive towards creation and far more compatible with the fundamental Christian world-view.

A sacrament, of course, embraces not only space, but also time. People tend not to live wholly in the present, which is the sacramental essence, as it relates to the presence of Christ in all times. We shall return to the notion of time as sacramental or eternal in the next section. Yet in regard to the environment, the sacramental principle relates to the presence of Christ in all places. Thus, the above contrast between the mechanistic and the more spiritual world-view is wonderfully described by Wendell Berry in relating the consequences of a very mundane event:

The figure representative of the earlier era was that of the otherworldly man who thought and said much more about where he would go when he died than about where he was living. Now we have the figure of the tourist-photographer who, one gathers, will never know where he is, but only, in looking at his pictures, where he was. Between his eye and the world is interposed the mechanism of the camera–and also, perhaps, the mechanism of economics: having bought the camera, he has to keep using it to get his money's worth. For him the camera will never work as an instrument of perception or discovery. Looking through it, he is not likely to see anything that will surprise or delight or frighten him, or change his sense of things. As he uses it, the camera is in bondage to the self-oriented assumptions that thrive within the social enclosure. It is an extension of his living room in which his pictures will finally be shown. And if you think the aspect or the atmosphere of his living room might be changed somewhat by the pictures of foreign places and wonders that he has visited then look, won't you, at the pictures themselves. He has photographed only what he has been prepared to see by other people's photographs. He has gone religiously and taken a picture of what he saw pictured in the travel brochures before he left home. He has photographed scenes that he could have bought on postcards or prepared slides at the nearest drugstore, the major difference being the frequent appearance in his photographs of himself, or his wife and children. He poses the members of his household on the brink of a canyon that the wind and water have been carving at for sixty million years as if there were an absolute equality between them, as if there were no precipice for the body and no abyss for the mind. And before he leaves he adds to the view his empty film cartons and the ruins of his picnic. He is blinded by the device by which he has sought to preserve his vision. He has, in effect, been no place and seen nothing; awesome wonders rest against his walls, deprived of mystery and immensity, reduced to his comprehension and his size, affirming his assumptions, as tame and predictable as a shelf of what nots.[1]

HISTORY AND HEAVEN

By the first century of the Christian era, Judaism had been profoundly infiltrated and influenced by Hellenism. The encounter of these two cultures and world-views had already been brought about after the rapid spread of Hellenism in the Palestinian and Alexandrian regions, particularly during the time of Alexander the Great and his successors. However, the Greek mind and the Biblical spirit were not totally compatible. The former sought truth in the harmony and beauty of the world, even if the material and historical were ultimately just an image of the spiritual and eternal. The latter searched for God in the immediacy of history, even if God is *the one who is and who was and who is [yet] to come* (Rev. 1:4). The early Christian community was in fact deeply marked by an eschatological orientation, by a sense of fervent expectation for the immediate and final revelation of God in history. Thus the early Church prayed *maranatha (i.e., the Lord is near)* whenever it celebrated the Eucharist.

Subsequently, the creative synthesis of the Greek interest in the cosmos and the Jewish sense of God's immanence emerges in the liturgical and monastic development of the Christian tradition. In the area of worship, the Church Fathers underlined the Eucharist as a foretaste of the final kingdom and as an act whereby material creation is transfigured by Christ.

In the area of the ascetic life, the Church Fathers played a crucial role of reconciliation in interpreting the function of the Church in the world (the community of believers as citizens of society: cf. Mark 12:17) and the goal of the Church not of this world (the Christian believers as citizens of heaven: cf. Heb. 13:14).

Another similar distinction is evident in the theological discourse of the first centuries. From the time of Tertullian (d.c.225),[2] theology in the Western part of Christendom has been characterized by a deep sense of *history* and the *historical*, of God working in time as we understand it, of an Aristotelian idea of beginning, middle, and end. This has resulted in a preoccupation with the institutional and the more "material" or moral aspects of Christianity. By contrast, Eastern theological thought has normally been concerned with the *metahistorical*, that is the *spiritual* dimensions of the Christian life seen in light of the kingdom of heaven and the eternal nature of time. The spirituality of the East has always searched for some ultimate theological reason behind and justification of historical events and situations. Facts and figures are interpreted in terms of the Holy Spirit; power is understood from the perspective of the sacrament of the Eucharist; the world around is considered in relation to the heaven above. This illuminating teaching about the Last Things, or the Last Times, has been at the forefront of theological and spiritual reflection.

To the minds of the early Christians, the "end" was far from any immediate concern for human life, as evidenced by the perception of the Church Fathers:

If the farmer waits all winter, so much more ought you to wait the final outcome of events, remembering who it is that ploughs the soil of our souls... And when I speak of the final outcome, I am not referring to the end of this present life, but to the future life and to God's plan for us, which aims at our salvation and glory.[3]

Unfortunately, most later theologians assumed that the Last Times (known in religious writings as *eschatology*) implied an apocalyptic or even an escapist attitude to the world. It took a long time even for these theologians to cease treating the Last Times as the last, perhaps unnecessary, chapter of Christian theology. Eschatology is not a teaching about the last things after everything else, but rather a teaching about the relation of all things to the *last things,* in essence about the *last-ness* and *lasting-ness* of all things. This is certainly how Gregory of Nyssa understood the beauty of this world, which was never intended for worship as an idol, as an end in itself:

since the conclusive harmony in the world has not yet been revealed.[4]

Gradually, however, the Omega has come to be interpreted as giving meaning to the Alpha, the eschatological vision of the present perceived as the way of liberation from the evils of provincialism and of narrow confessionalism, and the sacrament of the Eucharist accepted as the only true concept of reality because of its being rooted in an eternal present. For, the ultimate purpose of all that exists–the end–is the eucharistic offering of all to the Creator. And that is also the beginning, the original principle of the entire creation. In order to appreciate this, we require:

an attitude of mind sustained by a constant awareness of an End intensely present and powerful in the here and now of our historical existence and which imbues this existence with meaning. When and where we are ready or bold enough to think and live consistently to the end, we reach out every time to that final boundary where our lives are transcended into life eternal, to the Lord of Time, and in so doing we are living eschatologically: our History becomes not merely a series of happenings but the disclosure and consummation of divine and human destiny, that is, apocalypse... Human existence remains a temporal existence; its temporal character, however, contains the seed of the Kingdom: it is destined to end from within through self-transcendence and thus "prepare" the coming of the Kingdom. It must end from within as well as from without. The end from without cannot but be destruction, but the End from within is "construction" or "reconstruction" and transfiguration. "Verily, verily I say unto you, that there are some of them that stand here, who shall not taste death, till they have seen the Kingdom of God come with power."[5]

This sense of time as eternal is very significant for grasping the notion of the world as sacrament. For, it is in the sacraments that the world not only looks back in historical time to the moment of creation and to the event of the Incarnation, but also looks forward in sacramental time to, and even anticipates the redemption and restoration of all things–of all humanity and of all matter–in Christ on the Last Day. In the sacraments, everything visible assumes an invisible dimension; everything created adopts an uncreated perspective; everything purely mundane becomes deeply mystical, for in addition to being timely, it is also rendered timeless.

WHOLENESS AND HOLINESS

Our times demand positive encounter. Negative responses always remain a temptation, but they constitute a heresy inasmuch as they *isolate* one part of the truth, which is what the Greek word for *heresy (airesis)* actually signifies. Nonetheless, there is a narrow path between the heresy of fanaticism and the heresy of relativism, but not so narrow (cf. Matt. 7:13) that it cannot include the whole world and the abundance of life. The broader, holistic outlook that accepts the land and the world as crucial to our relationship with God bespeaks a reverence for the Holy Spirit and illustrates the connection between wholeness and holiness. If one can visualize the activity of the Spirit in nature, one can perceive the consubstantiality between humanity and the created order, and will no longer envisage humanity as the crown of a creation it is able to subdue. To regard the world without reference to the action of the Holy Spirit is to regard a philosophical, transcendent God incapable of being involved with human hearts and history. Only an unreserved affirmation of the Holy Spirit permits us to understand how God *moves out* of himself and enters into creation without disrupting divine unity or abandoning divine transcendence. We shall return to this theme in chapter four.

Affirming the action of the Holy Spirit also safeguards the intrinsically sacred character of creation, its sacramental dimension. For a sacrament remains, in all its transcendence, an historical event, demanding material expression. With God manifest in time and space, and the Eucharist as God's revelation in bread and wine, the world becomes the historical and material sacrament of the presence of God, transcending the ontological gap between created and uncreated. The world relates in very tangible terms the cooperation between divine and human in history, denoting the presence of God in our midst. Were God not present in the density of a city, or in the beauty of a forest, or in the sand of a desert, then God would not be present in heaven either.

Nature speaks a truth scarcely heard among theologians. In our minds, we have eliminated or excluded the role of created nature as central to the salvation of the world. I say *in our minds* advisedly, because if God is revealed in the created world, then God is present *in all things* (Col. 3:11). In other words, there is an invisible dimension to all things visible, a *beyond* to everything material. All creation is a palpable mystery, an immense *incarnation* of cosmic proportions. To C.S. Lewis, it is as if the Word was written out in large letters across the body of the world–in letters too large for us to read clearly. Augustine's celebrated phrase about himself in his *Confessions* might accordingly be expanded to state that God is *the most intimate interior and the supreme summit* of the whole world.[6]

A THEOLOGY OF CREATION

The word *sacrament* (from the Latin word *sacramentum)* can signify either a result or a means of consecration. The word was originally used in the third century Latin West as the equivalent of the Greek term *mystery (mysterion),* denoting a reality that is hidden but is gradually revealed through initiation *(myesis).* In the sense that everything in the cosmos in some way reflects the divine, the actual number of sacraments or mysteries cannot be limited to seven, still less to two or three. The sacramental principle is the way that we may understand the world around us as being sacred. This essential Christian vision consists of three fundamental intuitions concerning creation. When one of these is either isolated or violated, the result is an unbalanced and destructive vision of the world.

The first is the intuition that the world is good, that the world was created by a loving Creator.[7] From the beginning of time, creation has personified the biblical words *and God saw that it was good* (Gen. 1:25). The Septuagint Greek word for *good* is *kalos,* which also means *beautiful* and is derived from the verb "to call," implying that the world has been called by God to become beautiful. In short, the world's vocation is beauty. Nothing is intrinsically evil. Except perhaps the refusal to see God's work as beautiful. The entire world has been created for our enjoyment. In St. John Chrysostom's words:

The creation is beautiful and harmonious, and God has made it all just for your sake. He has made it beautiful, grand, varied, and rich.[9]

In a naive acceptance of this world-view, one would surrender to the world on the terms of the world and embrace a spirituality that assumes the conditions and criteria of a world that is absolutized–i.e., reduced to and rendered the only reality. Those who would secularize Christianity need to be reminded that there is an incalculable cost for the process of cosmic transfiguration because of the reality of evil. The glory of Mt. Tabor cannot be separated from the suffering of Mt. Calvary; the two hills are spiritually complementary, because creation *groans* and *travails* in search of and in expectation of deliverance (cf. Rom 8:22).

The second intuition is the understanding that the world is also evil. This more negative alternative affirms that creation is fallen, that the world lies entirely within the realm of the prince of evil. The results of this *fall* are inevitably felt also on the level of the created world. This should not surprise us, writes John Chrysostom:

Why should you be surprised that the human race's wickedness can hinder the fertility of the earth? For our sake the earth was subjected to corruption, and for our sake it will be free of it... Its being like this or that has its roots in this destiny. We see proof of this in the story of Noah... What happens to the world, happens to it for the sake of the dignity of the human race.[10]

This intuition might explain, at least in part, the radical dualism of the Manicheans and Gnostics in the early Christian Church, according to whom the visible creation has not fallen from perfection, but is the work of an inferior deity. This alternative is not always expressed so crudely: it may be that the world is regarded as merely a stage for the more important human drama to be played out. This almost *apocalyptic* world-view dictates withdrawal or escape from the created world, followed by an inevitable condemnation of the vast majority of humanity who wallow in this *inferior* creation and a belief in the salvation only of *the few.* Furthermore, this pietism isolates a narrow band of human experience as *sacred,* while all else is relegated to the realm of the *secular.* The goal, however, is not to set the sacramental over, against, or even outside, the *profane* part of life, but to realize that nothing is intrinsically non-sacred (cf. Mark 7:19 and Rom. 14:14), that nothing is excluded from the sacramental principle. But by the same token, we must emphasize that because everything is fallen, absolutely everything requires transformation.

The third intuition is the belief that affirms the world as redeemed. The Incarnation, Crucifixion and Resurrection of Jesus Christ effected the recreation of the world. This redemption, however, can only be fully appreciated in light of the other two intuitions of reality that were mentioned above: createdness and fallenness. Otherwise, the emphasis on human progress and achievement, together with the optimistic development of civilization, will lead us to the post-Christian determinism that has influenced much of Western technology and culture during the last centuries. The result would be a renunciation of the center of Christian faith, that liberation from sin and transformation of evil are wrought by God both in the unique nature of creation and in the total assumption of creation at the divine Incarnation. Human salvation and cosmic transfiguration can only be achieved by cooperation between Creator and creation, not by an imposition of one over the other.

The *honest to God* and the *death of God* debates of the sixties brought about a total devotion to the world and to its concerns, as well as a total resistance to any self-centered individualism or pietism. Theologians in those years alerted us to the danger of disenchanting nature, of stripping it of any mysterious quality. *This disenchantment of the natural world provides an absolute precondition for the development of natural science... and makes nature itself available for man's use.*[11]

Today's lack of regard for and detachment from God's creation could be signs of indifference towards the world and its goodness or a refusal to engage with its fallen aspects. Any definition of the proper Christian attitude towards the world must involve some form of synthesis, a dialectical approach that reflects the nature of reality as a world of *opposites.* The world is both *good* and *fallen,* and these opposites are rooted in revelation and in the experience of the Church. And so the world emerges as a sacrament, at least in the mystical and ascetical traditions of the Orthodox Church, and the relationship of humanity to the environment is perceived in sacramental terms.

SACRAMENT AND SYMBOL

Ironically, it is the paradoxical or antinomical character of creation understood as sacrament which preserves the balance between the two aforementioned world-views and dismisses the slightest suspicion of theism or pantheism. For a sacrament can be a symbol of both the transcendence and the immanence of God, transcendence implying not divine aloofness but active involvement, ecstatic[12] dynamism. Sacraments therefore reveal not only the dimension of depth but also the abyss of mystery in God, recalling not an absent God but One who is present everywhere.

When we refer to a sacrament as symbol, we must rid ourselves of the notion that symbols are merely reminders or signs, which symbolize something else or have an ulterior meaning. The ultimate significance of the symbol is its gratuitousness, almost its *uselessness:* it quite simply means, and does not mean something else.

This of course is a difficult concept to grasp in a world that expects what-you-see-is-what-you-get productivity and *usefulness,* in a world that measures everything in terms of consumer value.

Creation as sacrament is symbolic, like life, art and poetry, with the symbol being understood in its original etymological sense of a *syn-drome* or an image that brings together *(sym-ballo)* two realities. Clearly certain symbols are more appropriate than others, particularly those which bear no apparent similarity with the archetype or original, since there can be no pretense or disguise of the archetype. The more veiling and distant the symbol, the greater the unveiling *(*the *apo-calypse* or *re-velation)* of the invisible God. Consequently, the earth becomes the very image of heaven, the ground revealing the abyss above, and the way we treat the world around us reflects our relationship with the God we worship. Our role is to dis-cover or un-cover–*at every hour and every moment, both in heaven and on earth,*[13] *in all places of God's dominion* (Psalm 103:22)–the inwardness of the outward, just as the mystics have done through the ages. For the *end* is already inaugurated among us, and the *there* may be foretasted in the here and now. A sacrament is that which reveals life and the world as a movement incorporating Alpha to Omega, as transition from old to new, as *Pascha* or passover from death to life.

That is not to say sacraments are isolated from the world or from people. Though open to the mysterious and eternal, they retain a material and temporal nature,

articulating divine glory that is present in all things. It is
we who often do not see clearly:

*If your eye is healthy, your whole body will be filled with
light* (Matt. 6:22).

Thus we are called to see paradoxical things in unity and
not in contradiction, a reconciliation, if you will, which
is brought about by art, literature, and religion:

*Who but Shakespeare could bring the airy nothing of
heaven into consonance with the heavy reality of earth,
and give it a form that ordinary humans can understand?
Who but the Shakespeare in yourself?... When one is
truly a citizen of both worlds, heaven and earth are no
longer antagonistic to each other... [It is] only the optical
illusion of our capacity–and need–to see things double.*[14]

Religion is a *re-relating,* a *re-binding (re-ligio),* whose
purpose is to put back together again, to heal the wounds
of separation. A religious insight to the world connects
and bridges by restoring and reconciling the apparent
opposites that cause us suffering and torment–the
neurosis, to use *therapeutical* jargon, caused by such
dualism.

Thus it is that in Orthodox spirituality, the ultimate
symbol or sacrament is the Divine Liturgy, constituting
as it does the celebration, perception and very presence
of heaven on earth. This is how the Eastern Orthodox
tradition presents a firm spiritual and intellectual

framework for a balanced affirmation of the holiness of this world. In the words of St. Symeon of Thessalonika (d. 1429), the Divine Liturgy constitutes *the mystery of mysteries... the holy of holies, the initiation of all initiations.*[15] And around the same time, St. Nicholas Cabasilas (d.c. 1391) commented:

This is the final mystery. Beyond this it is not possible to go, nor can anything be added to it.[16]

"CREATION OUT OF NOTHING"

We have already noted that, according to the Judaeo-Christian tradition, the world was created "out of nothing," namely for no other reason than for God's unconditional love. Creation *out of nothing (ex nihilo)* is not part of the Genesis story, but is a doctrine which emerged in the inter-testamental period, the earliest reference being found in the book of Maccabees (II Macc. 7:28), and therefore not available to the writers of the Hebrew Scriptures. It was entirely unknown to the world of classical philosophy during the pre-Christian and early Christian times, and emerged slowly and uncertainly within Christian theology as a response to Greek cosmology. Tertullian expresses this vagueness in the second century:

I say that, although Scripture did not clearly proclaim that all things were made out of nothing–just as it does not say either that they were made out of matter–there was not so great a need to declare that all things had been made out of nothing as there would have been, if they were made out of matter.[17]

The doctrine of creation out of nothing first assumes prominence in the subsequent Christian tradition[18] to safeguard creation as an act of freedom and not of necessity, as a product of love and not of nature, a result of will and not of essence. Indeed by the early fourth century there is agreement, among orthodox and heretical writers alike. At the Council of Nicea (325), the first ecumenical council which generally marks a watershed in the history of Christian thought, Athanasius and Arius–opponents on many other issues–share a clearly articulated doctrine of creation out of nothing. The former lists and subsequently rejects the possible alternatives, clearly contrasting the uncreated Creator with the created order:

In regard to the making of the universe and the creation of all things there have been various opinions, and each person has propounded the theory that suited his own taste. For instance, some say that all things are self-originated and, so to speak, haphazard. The Epicureans are among these; they deny that there is any Mind behind the universe at all. This view is contrary to all the facts of experience, their own existence included... Others take the view expressed by Plato, that giant among the Greeks. He said that God had made all things out of pre-existent and uncreated matter, just as the carpenter makes things only out of wood that already exists. But those who hold this view do not realize that to deny that

God is himself the Cause of matter is to impute limitation to him, just as it is undoubtedly a limitation on the part of the carpenter that he can make nothing unless he has the wood. How could God be called Maker and Artificer if his ability to make depended on some other cause, namely on matter itself? If he only worked up existing matter and did not himself bring matter into being, he would be not the Creator but only a craftsman.

Then, again, there is the theory of the Gnostics, who have invented for themselves an Artificer of all things other than the Father of our Lord Jesus Christ. These simply shut their eyes to the obvious meaning of Scripture... St. John, speaking all-inclusively, says, "All things became by him and without him came nothing into being." How then could the Artificer be someone different, other than the Father of Christ?

Such are the notions which people put forward. But the impiety of their foolish talk is plainly declared by the divine teaching of the Christian faith. From it we know that, because there is Mind behind the universe, it did not originate itself; because God is infinite, not finite, it was not made from pre-existent matter, but out of nothing and out of non-existence, absolute and utter, God brought it into being through the Word. ...For God is good–or rather, of all goodness he is Fountainhead, and it is impossible for one who is good to be mean or grudging about anything. Grudging existence to none, therefore, he made all things out of nothing through his own Word, our Lord Jesus Christ.[19]

Athanasius refers to earlier Christian authorities as well as to Scripture in order to distinguish between the Trinitarian relationship of the Father to the Son (which he describes in one word as *gennesis*, or *birth)* and the relationship of the Son within the Trinity to the world (which again in one term he describes as *genesis*, or *creation*). The ultimate *problem* with such a definitive and ontological distinction between God and the world is that there is no intermediate zone between the two. The only exception, as we have seen, is the sacrament of the Eucharist. The implications and conclusions from this doctrinal formulation are dramatic not only for theology (as being the understanding of God), but also for cosmology (as being the understanding of the world) and for mystical theology (as being the experience of God in the world).[20]

GOD AND THE WORLD

In some pagan creation myths, both matter and the divine beings assume eternal existence. The Christian Church, by contrast, believes God alone is the eternal being, *maker of all things visible and invisible* (Nicene Creed). The distinction is that God is omnipotent and independent, while the world is limited, dependent, and always understood in reference to and in communion with God, without whom it is incomplete.

The inherent danger of the Christian doctrine is the temptation to press the sovereign independence of God to the point of separation from the world. No one is today threatened by any form of *deism,* by a God entirely unrelated to the world, preferring to speak in terms of *theism,* of a God related and relevant to our world. Yet we are reluctant to advance this relatedness any further, lest we be criticized of *pan-theism.* Some prefer to speak of *pan-en-theism,* in order to ensure some safe distinction between God and the world. However this term is neither always clear in meaning nor always consistent in usage, inasmuch as it is adopted by thinkers and theologians of all persuasions.

The question now arises as to the precise content of the *nothing (nihil)* from which God creates: is it an emptiness that is deprived of God? Or is it that it is nothing inasmuch as it represents the energies of God?[21] The Western mystic Eriugena noted that *nihil* is another name for God, an alternative description for the ultimate abyss of the divinity. And the notion is not unknown in the Eastern mystics, which is perhaps where Eriugena received and repeated it.

In his work *On Divine Names,* Dionysius the Areopagite refers to God as being:

at one and the same time in the world (encosmic), and around the world (pericosmic), and above the world (hypercosmic)...as being everything and nothing... Nothing contains and comprehends God...and nothing exists that does not share in God.[22]

The same understanding is also found in the spiritual teaching of a more contemporary Orthodox Saint, John of Kronstadt, who was a parish priest and spiritual director in Russia:

The Lord fills all creation... preserving it down to the smallest blade of grass and grain of dust in his right hand, and not being limited either by the greatness or smallness of things created; he exists in infinity, entirely filling it, as a vacuum...[23]

Therefore, the *nothing* from which God creates is not the absence of God, but is in fact another way of denoting the presence of God. Contemporary physics supports such a view of matter as nothingness. This is the spirituality of the *sponge* that is promoted in the fourteenth century by such writers as St. Gregory Palamas, who uses this image to describe the way in which God's energies permeate human and material nature.[24] Seen through the eyes of a physicist, the human body itself is 99.99 per cent void, and even the little that appears to be dense matter is itself empty space. The whole thing is made out of nothing. Think of creation *ex nihilo* as a form of "quantum" theology or spirituality that holds together the absence and the presence of God in the world.

GOD AS TRANSCENDENT AND IMMANENT

An emphasis, therefore, is definitely given to the transcendence of God, but in the radical otherness of

God, the oneness of God in relation to the world is maintained, even though the temptation remains to divide God from the world. Creation out of nothing, as a central Christian doctrine, needs to be considered in light of the essential Orthodox doctrine of the distinction between divine essence (that is totally unknowable) and divine energies (that constitute God's revelation and reflection in the world), which will be explored more fully in the next chapter. Together, these two teachings refute the notions that the material world exists independently of God (dualism) and that it is identical to God (pantheism).

The Bible also appears to lay greater stress on the transcendence of God and on the dependence of humanity or the world upon God. There is less emphasis on separation and independence between the two. Creation is never considered to be self-sufficient. Nonetheless, the gap between Creator and creation is not irreconcilable, even for Scripture, which endeavors to hold the two together in a couple of ways. First, there is the two-fold interpretation of creation with the use of two distinct Hebraic verbs.[25] Second, there is the attempt of the Hebraic tradition to preserve the immanence of God and the extensive relationship between God and the world through the quality of divine *image and likeness* (Gen. 1:26) according to which humanity was created. It is because God has a face that the world too has a face, and eyes, and a voice; and it is because humanity has a face that it is able to discern the face of God in the face of the world.[26]

At this point, a parenthetical remark should be made to correct the unbalanced reference, or reduction, of this *image and likeness* to the spiritual or rational aspect of humanity. Unfortunately the indivisible unity of the human person has often been undergirded in Christian thought, although this was not the case in scriptural literature. Similarly, for the Greek Fathers, the human person always retained an element of mystery, due largely to the belief in the human person as an irreducible being consisting of body, soul, and spirit.

The world, therefore, reflects the beauty and glory and unity of its Creator. *The heavens tell the glory of God, and the firmament proclaims God's handiwork* (Psalm 18:1). The whole of creation comprises *a mystical harmony that constitutes a song of praise.*[27] Despite its unity and beauty, creation is not unidimensional. Instead it reveals a loving God that cooperates in a relationship of Trinity in order to create. It is this love of God (cf. I John 4:16) which undergirds the relationship of humanity with the rest of creation. The Orthodox wedding ceremony underlines this link between creation, beauty, and union:

O God, you have in your strength created all things, established the universe, and adorned the crown of all things created by you... Blessed is your name and glorified is your kingdom: Father, Son, and Holy Spirit.

Again we must disabuse ourselves of a commonplace misinterpretation of the Old Testament command: *Be fruitful and multiply; and fill the earth and subdue it; and have dominion over...every living thing that moves upon the earth* (Gen. 1:28). For centuries this text has provided the license to dominate and abuse the world according to our selfish needs and purposes. Yet how can such an interpretation ever be reconciled with Paul's advice in the New Testament, that we are to *use the world without abusing it* (I Cor. 7:31)? The Genesis passage should instead be understood in the context of Adam's naming of the animals as described in chapter five:

So out of the ground the Lord God formed every animal of the field and every bird of the air, and brought them to the man to see what he would call them; and whatever the man called every living creature, that was its name. The man gave names to all cattle, and to the birds of the air, and to every animal of the field... (Gen. 2: 19-20).

This event implies a loving and lasting personal relationship on the part of Adam with the environment, indicative of the same dialectical (literally *in dialogue)* relationship between Adam and his Creator.[28] The radical de-divinization of the world, wrought by our inability to maintain a relationship with God, may cause our lack of caring responsibility towards both heaven and earth. The *dominion* of humanity over the world must in fact always be interpreted in light of human responsibility towards nature, whereby one is called to care for the land (cf. Levit. 25:1-5), for domesticated animals (cf. Deut. 25:4), and even for wild life (cf. Deut. 22:6). We fall short of that vocation when we fail to care for creation. In fact, we sin by refusing that call, for the world remains a wasteland unless it comes alive. And it comes alive by the act of a vital human who becomes the conscience, the eyes, the voice, the ears of the earth.

So the world, while constituting a different and distinct reality from God, nevertheless remains a revelation of the personal and creative uniqueness of God. This revelation, at times silent and other times blatant, manifests an inviolable relationship with its Creator.[29] Furthermore, the different and distinct reality of the world constitutes the only premise and promise for this relationship with God.

THE MYSTERY OF INCARNATION

A sacramental consciousness–a recognition of and respect for the sacramental principle–requires an awareness of the centrality of the Incarnation in its historical, spiritual, and cosmic senses. Eastern Christian writers have viewed the Incarnation more as a normative spiritual movement than as an isolated moment. Gregory of Nyssa, for instance, uses terms such as *sequence (eirmos), consequence (akolouthia)*, or–his favorite –*progression (epektasis)*. That is to say, God always and in all things wills to work a divine incarnation. The Word assuming flesh two thousand years ago is one–though arguably the last, and even the most striking–in a series of incarnations or theophanies. For, divine self-emptying *(kenosis:* cf. Phil. 2:7) into the world is an essential, and not an exceptional, characteristic of God. In fact, it is a call to humanity and creation for transformation:

He [Christ] emptied himself, so that nature might receive as much of him as it could hold.[30]

Furthermore, the Incarnation is considered as part of the original creative plan, and not simply as a response to the human fall. In this regard, it is perceived not only as a revelation of God to humanity but primarily as a revelation to us of the true nature of humanity and the world itself. Such is the line of thought of Isaac the Syrian in the East and of Duns Scotus (thirteenth century) in the West. This is also the basic theological focus of Maximus Confessor, who insists on the reality of Christ's presence in all things (cf. Col. 3:11). Christ is the one who stands at the center of the world, revealing its original beauty and restoring its ultimate life.

The Incarnation is thus properly understood only in relation to creation. The Word made flesh is intrinsic to the very act of creation, which came to be through God's uttering or divine Word.[31] Cosmic Incarnation is, in some manner, independent of the historical incarnation of two thousand years ago. From the moment of creation, the world is assumed by the Word and constitutes the body of this Word. The historical Incarnation is in effect a re-affirmation of this reality, and not an alteration of reality. Indeed, according to the first letter of Peter:

Christ...was destined before the foundation of the world, but was revealed at the end of the ages for our sakes (I Peter 1:20).

From the moment of its creation, the world is the living body of the divine Logos. For *God spoke the word (logos) and things were made, God commanded and they were created* (Psalm 33:9). Thus creation may be regarded as a continuous process where the divine Logos is manifested in time and space according to the particular personal energies. The Incarnation then assumes a cosmological, and not simply an historical, significance. This is already intimated in the fourth century by Athanasius who is unafraid of broadening these implications of the doctrine on the Incarnation of Christ:

And more strange, being Logos, he is not constrained by anything; rather he himself constrains everything; and just as being in the whole of creation, he is on the one hand outside everything according to essence but within everything with his powers, setting all in order, and extending in every way his providence to everything, and vivifying alike each and every thing, embracing all and not himself embraced, but being wholly and in every way in his Father alone, and in this manner also being in the human body, and himself vivifying it, he likewise vivifies all and is in everything even while he is outside everything.[32]

LOGOS AND LOGOI

Christ is the new Adam who realizes the sacrament that was rejected by us. But if we turn around from the world of darkness and accept to live in Christ, then each person and each object is the embodiment of God in the world. The divine Presence is revealed to every order and particle of this world; the divine Word [or *Logos*] converses intimately with the word [or *logos*] of creation. For the divine Logos always and everywhere *wills to effect this mystery of his embodiment.*[33] This of course implies a contemplation of the principles *(logoi)* of creation, an insight into the meanings *(logoi)* and causes *(logoi)* of the world, a vision of the flesh and blood of Christ in the soil of the earth and the cells of matter. Such a vision is already expressed in the Alexandrian tradition by Philo and, later, by Origen who envisioned the eternal Logos being manifested in history and in the world under various guises:

There exist diverse forms of the Logos, under which he reveals himself to his disciples, conforming himself to the degree of light in each one, according to the degree of their progress in saintliness.[34]

Maximus Confessor refers to these divine logoi as being *conceived* only in the eternal Logos of God, constituted by the Son and instituted by the Spirit in historical time and place. We might speak of an *uncreated createdness* of all things, which pre-exist in God's will (or *logos*), and are brought by the divine will into existence and being:

He conceals himself mysteriously in the interior causes (logoi) of created beings...present in each totally and in all his plenitude;...in all diversity is concealed that which is one and eternally identical; in composite things, that which is simple and without parts; in those which had one day to begin that which has no beginning; in the visible that which is invisible; in the tangible that which is intangible.[35]

However, the words *(logoi)* of creation demand deciphering. The *Macarian Homilies* speak of interpreting the language spoken by creation.[36] They require silence in order to hear and to dialogue *(dia-logos)* with the Word *(Logos)* of the Creator. The incarnate Word of God is the basis of harmony and union, while sin and division blur our vision of everything as proclaiming the beauty of God. As pre-eternal Word, the Son of God is the giver of this gift; and as incarnate Word, Jesus Christ is the receiver of this gift. The Orthodox liturgical rite summarizes this in the words of Basil the Great:

For you, Christ our God, are the one who offers and is offered, the one who receives and is received...

The Word of God is the one who relates and reconciles the world to God:

In relation to the benevolent, creative and sustaining progress of the One towards created things, the One is multiple (Unum est multa); but considered in relation to the return of things and their tendency towards the principle sustaining all things, the Center who has by anticipation in himself the beginnings of all the lines which have come from him, considered in this aspect, the multiple are One (multa sunt Unum).[37]

This unity is confirmed in the joy of creation and is celebrated in the liturgy of the Church. In this way, the Church becomes an image of the world, just as the world bespeaks a cosmic liturgy. For the ecclesial vision of the world in Maximus Confessor (d. 660), the Church represents the world and the world reflects the Church in, as he calls it, microcosm.[38] The sense of heaven reflected on earth is nowhere more evident than in the splendid architecture and symbolic liturgy of the Byzantine churches, especially that of the *Hagia Sophia* (the Church of the Holy Wisdom) in Constantinople. For, when Orthodox Christians enter a Church, they are in the comfort of their own home, and when they leave the building of the Church, the feeling is that they are still inside the Church because the whole world is identified with the Church. Indeed, the world is called to do more than merely to reflect or represent the Church. It is supposed to respect and reveal the unified structure of the Body of Christ, transcending all divisions between created and uncreated, heaven and earth, paradise and world, as well as between male and female.[39]

THE MYSTERY OF THE CROSS AND THE RESURRECTION

The ascetic attitude towards the world and the body seems to discourage subjective domination over objects. Everything is required to undergo crucifixion in order to achieve resurrection; everything must die in order to rise (cf. John 12:24-25). Or, in the words again of Maximus Confessor, himself an ascetic and monastic, *all phenomena must be crucified.*[40] Like Christ, everything requires incarnation (materiality), crucifixion (testing through the fire of death, by being raised to the vertical level of God), descent into hell (and to the deepest and darkest recesses of the heart), before it can arise in the light and life of Christ. It is what the Greek Fathers like to call *the little Resurrection* (for example, Evagrius of Pontus, d.399) or *the resurrection before the Resurrection* (for example, John Climacus, d.c. 649). We read of the radiance of the elderly Seraphim of Sarov who greeted his visitors with the salutation of Easter: *My joy, Christ is risen.* We cannot forget, of course, the long, hard years of physical struggle, solitude, and silence that precede any such Resurrection. The Christian ascetic tradition, in its more authentic expressions, perceives the Cross more as a way of transforming the world than a means of tolerating it (as in the case of the Cynic philosophers).

The Orthodox liturgical tradition combines this scandalous mystery of the Cross with the luminous majesty of the Resurrection–the Crucifixion prepares the Resurrection, while the Resurrection presupposes the Crucifixion. Together they effect the redemption and sanctification of the whole world. Thus on Good Friday, the Orthodox sing:

All the trees of the forest rejoice today. For their nature is sanctified by the body of Christ stretched on the wood [of the Cross].

On Easter Sunday the celebration reaches a climax:
Now everything is filled with the light [of the Resurrection]: heaven and earth, and all things beneath the earth.

Athanasius of Alexandria understood this universal dimension:

Christ is the foretaste of the Resurrection of all...the first-fruits of the adoption of all creation...the first-born of the whole world in its every aspect.[41]

In the Resurrection of Jesus Christ, in the abyss of an empty tomb and in the depth of joy of the mystical encounters between the risen Lord and his disciples, both women and men, the inner meaning of creation is revealed and discovered. In a sense, the Genesis account of creation can only be understood in the light of the Resurrection *that enlightens every person coming into the world* (John 1:9). Through the Resurrection one perceives the end and intent of God (cf. Prov. 8:31); one senses in Christ a new creation, a new earth, and a new joy. Thus Jesus is recognized (cf. Luke 24:31) as the meaning and life of the whole world, and not simply as the moral redeemer of individual souls. To him belongs the entire creation, and in him one discovers the destiny of creation. For *he came to what was his own* (John 1:11). He came:

to make everyone see what is the plan of the mystery hidden for ages in God who created all things, so that...the wisdom of God in its rich variety might now be made known...in accordance with the eternal purpose that God has carried out in Jesus Christ our Lord (Eph. 3:9-11).

The two feast days of the early Christian Church that signify new life and new lights are Easter and Epiphany (January 6), and these were the primary baptismal days for those wishing to be received into the Church. The Orthodox Church today still preserves these powerful images of resurrection and regeneration, and the services for these feasts abound in images expressing the way in which the entire universe and all created matter contribute to the cosmic liturgy:

Now everything is filled with light, heaven and earth, and all things beneath the earth; so let all creation celebrate the Resurrection of Christ on which it is founded.[42]

Today creation is illumined; today all things rejoice, everything in heaven and on earth.[43]

Today the earth and the sea share in the joy of the world.[44]

It is not by chance that both of these central feasts of the Orthodox Church underline the creation of the world *in the first days* (cf. Gen. 1) and understand the significance of the re-creation accomplished *in the latter days* (cf. Heb. 1:2) in light of the restoration of all things *in the last days* (cf. II Tim. 3:1).

THE ASCETIC DIMENSION

The Christian takes seriously the reality and the tragic dimension of evil. Christianity describes the world as it should be, refusing to accept it as it is. Thus, all expressions of pantheism and paganism have from the earliest years been refuted and refused. Furthermore, the sacrament of initiation, Baptism, is preceded by a long series of exorcisms: of the individual, of the world around, and of the water of baptism itself. In the East, the *sin of Adam* is understood in the East as *the fall* from life to mere survival, with its chief consequence being mortality and corruption, not guilt. Death is therefore seen as a cosmic disease that infects humanity and all of creation, its reversal effected through Baptism which is a participation in the Resurrection of Christ, a real communion in his victory over death. According to Maximus, the world was created as a dynamic movement,[45] and this movement towards transfiguration in the light of the Resurrection is its very *raison d' être*.

There is, then, no greater estrangement from the world than its use in a manner that fails to restore the correct vision of the world in the light of the Resurrection. Any other vision is an abuse of the world. We have *exchanged the truth...for a lie...and the natural use of things for an unnatural abuse* (cf. Rom. 1:25-26). As such, the discipline of *ascesis* becomes a crucial corrective for the excess of consumption. For we have learned all too well and all too painfully that the ecological crisis both presupposes and builds upon the economic abuse and injustice in the world.

Now when Orthodox Christianity refers to asceticism, it is not implying an individualistic or puritanistic life of self-discipline, nor is it promulgating an idealistic or sentimentalistic form of deprivation. Asceticism is regarded as a *social* event; it is a communal attitude that leads to the respectful use of material goods. The underlying conviction is that we are never alone, never isolated from one another and from our earth of origin (cf. Gen. 3 and Psalm 102:14). The Old Testament prophets warned us against this kind of social indifference and injustice, which is epitomized by consumption:

Ah, you who join house to house, and add field to field, until there is room for no one but you, and you are left alone in the midst of the land (Isaiah 5:8).

Ascesis implies spiritual development without violating the personal limitations of others. It also involves terrestrial development without exceeding the environmental sustainability of the earth.

Therefore, in spite of all historical and human aberrations (and Christians have often been the primary culprits for the scars on the beauty of both the human body, as well as on the body of the world), what is in fact avoided in authentic ascetic practice is not so much *the world, or the things in the world...*[*but*] *the desire of the flesh and the lust of the eyes and the pride in riches* (I John 2:15-16). *Flesh* of course signifies the whole of one's life in the state of conflict with oneself, with the world, and with

God. *Lust of the eyes* implies the blurred vision of the world as created and as intended by God. *Pride* constitutes the ultimate hubris of humanity that usurps the role of God and seeks to dominate the world.

The various expressions of the religious or monastic life sometimes deviate into a form of *angelism* that verges on the point of disincarnation and dematerialization in its aggressive attitude towards the body. Yet the ascetic life, at least in its more authentic expression, is a way of tenderness and of integration with oneself, with each other and with creation. The genuine Christian ascetic is the universal person who is freed from narrowness and limitations and divisions. The vision of the ascetic is both visual and personal: they are consciously aware that the problem of pollution cannot be distinguished from the problem of inner alienation. In the way to transfiguration, the Christian ascetic by no means leaves creation outside but in fact unites the whole cosmos discarded by sin.

In his Epistles, St. Paul speaks of a certain division or dualism between *flesh* and *spirit,* but never does he intimate that there should be any separation or severance between body and soul or between humanity and the material world. Later Christian writers commonly fail to observe this distinction. For Paul, matter is not an enemy to be conquered, but rather a means whereby one can glorify the Creator. *The flesh is the hinge of salvation,* wrote Tertullian.[46] And so transfiguration through asceticism entails the revelation of the spiritual potentiality of the world and not its suppression. Rather than latent dualism, one may discover the exact opposite in the austerities of the desert ascetics. This will be examined in detail in the following section, but here let it be said that transfiguration in *ascesis* foreshadows the ultimate resurrection, being in this life the first fruits of cosmic redemption and resurrection. Through ascetic toil, the monastic recognizes and responds to the brightness of all people and all things. Indeed, through *ascesis*, nature itself responds more compassionately toward humanity, as St. John of Kronstadt writes:

When God looks mercifully upon the earth-born creatures through the eyes of nature, through the eyes of bright, healthful weather, everyone feels bright and joyful... So powerful and irresistible is the influence of nature upon mankind. And it is remarkable that those who are less bound by carnal desires and sweetness, who are less given up to gluttony, who are more moderate in eating and drinking; to them nature is more kindly disposed, and does not oppress them–at least, not nearly so much as those who are slaves of their nature and flesh.[47]

This is the only way of reality. For, in the words of Gregory the Theologian (329-c.390), *to detach oneself from matter is to cease to be human.*[48] A philosophy of disembodiment, of dematerialization and of separation is a philosophy of death. Extreme asceticism and excessive spiritualism alike represent a partial truth; and to assert these in isolation is to destroy the harmony of the world.

Therefore, the ascetic aspect in any ecological and theological awareness is not the result of escape from the world or of any abstract thinking. Rather, it is the reassurance of our difficult and painful struggle to relate our theology to the world, our justice to the oppressed, and our economy to the poor.

THE SEED OF GOD

It is a tragedy that, in spite of the destruction caused and the suffering inflicted, we have not yet apparently learned the lesson. We are still far from a balanced perspective of creation as deriving from, dependent upon, and deified by God. The world remains a human-centered reality, indeed, it is still more narrowly conceived as man-centered. We are preoccupied at all times with ourselves, with our problems, our destructiveness, our death. And yet this is precisely what has led us in the first place to this fateful predicament. Priority is given to humanity (in fact particularly to the human spirit, or even the human reason) as the center of creation. Human reason examines and exploits nature and matter; human reason decides upon the relatedness and relevance of the various parts of the world; and human reason uses and abuses creation through domination.

Contemporary *deep ecology* emphasizes the fact that the correct perspective and relationship between humanity and creation has been distorted, almost destroyed. Yet little significance is attached to the reality that all things are coherent not just in their interrelatedness and interdependence, but also in their relation to and dependence on God. In fact, to be estranged from God is to lose touch also with created reality and with what really matters in this world. It is to be enslaved within the vicious cycle of death and destruction. Symeon the New Theologian expressed this in poetry in tenth-century Constantinople:

What is more painful than to be separated from Life?...
For it also means to miss out on all good things. The one
that moves away from God loses all that is good.[49]

And according to an earlier, fourth-century poet and theologian of the same city, Gregory Nazianzus:

All things dwell in God alone; to God all things throng in
haste. And God is the end of all things.[50]

The ancient Greeks too had a similar world-view, discerning the presence of God in all things. Thales exclaimed:

Everything is full of God.[51]

In their cosmology, the transcendence of God was perceived as a characteristic that rendered the divinity more accessible and more familiar. The slightest detail of creation was seen to bear *some mark of the Creator:*

Look at a stone, and notice that even a stone carries
some mark of the Creator. It is the same with an ant, a

bee, a mosquito. The wisdom of the Creator is revealed in the smallest creatures. It is he who has spread out the heavens and laid out the immensity of the seas. It is he also who has made the tiny hollow shaft of the bee's sting. All the objects in the world are an invitation to faith, not to unbelief.[52]

The same theological truth is also expressed outside of established theology and poetry. The well-known Greek writer of this century, Nikos Kazantzakis, experienced a tumultuous life, and his works caused tumult among pious believers who misunderstood him. Yet he has a powerful religious vision of the seed of God in the world. This helps in understanding the theological notion of the connection between the divine *Logos* and the *logoi* in creation. For seed requires a specific soil, some earth on which to be sown and in which to grow.[53] And a seed also requires an almost cosmic passion for its cultivation. The Little Prince knows that:

seeds are invisible. They sleep deep in the heart of the earth's darkness, until some one among them is seized with the desire to awaken.[54]

This is the kind of passion displayed and described by Kazantzakis. His book *Ascetic Exercises* describes in a compelling manner this same relationship among God, the world, and us:

Everything is an egg, and within it lies the seed of God, calmlessly and sleeplessly active... Within the light of my mind and the fire of my heart, I beset God's watch–searching, testing, knocking to open the door in the stronghold of matter, and to create in that stronghold of matter, the door of God's heroic exodus... For we are not simply freeing God in struggling with and ordering the visible world around us; we are actually creating God. Open your eyes, God is crying; I want to see! Be alert; I want to hear! Move ahead; you are my head!... For to save something [a rock or a seed] is to liberate the God within it... Every person has a particular circle of things, of trees, of animals, of people, of ideas–and the aim is to save that circle. No one else can do that. And if one doesn't save, one cannot be saved... The seeds are calling out from inside the earth; God is calling out from inside the seeds. Set him free. A field awaits liberation from you, and a machine awaits its soul from you. And you can no longer be saved, if you don't save them... The value of this transient world is immense and immeasurable: it is from this world that God hangs on in order to reach us; it is in this world that God is nurtured and increased... Matter is the bride of my God: together they struggle, they laugh and mourn, crying through the nuptial chamber of the flesh. [55]

CHAPTER FOUR

Divine Immanence and Divine Transcendence

EARLY CHRISTIANITY AND THE MIDDLE AGES

GOD AND THE WORLD

When one begins to have a conceptual awareness of God as being sacred, and of divine action in the world as being sacramental, one becomes aware of the dialectical, almost paradoxical character of God's presence in creation: on the one hand, a sense of affinity or immanence whereby God is recognizable in the beauty of the world; and on the other hand a sense of otherness or transcendence, whereby God is above and beyond anything worldly.

This chapter examines select thinkers and theologians from the early Christian and medieval times, who have been influential on the contemporary world, in order to see how they perceived creation. The aim is to foster an historical appreciation of inherited concepts, both eastern and western, positive and negative alike. I have tried not to present here many of the authors referred to in earlier and later chapters, but to introduce less familiar writers who were greatly influential on the development of Christian thought and practice, and in particular on Christian attitudes toward creation.

CLEMENT OF ALEXANDRIA (c.150-c.215)
–THE ORDER OF THE WORLD

During the second and third centuries, the world's intellectual and cultural center, Alexandria, also came to be recognized as the capital of Hellenism. It was there that Jewish and Christian traditions came into contact with the Greek world. Although the Church in Alexandria did not boast excessively of any apostolic sources, its origins are indeed very early, but the peculiarity of Alexandria in fact lay in its *school.* In contrast with the institutional authority of bishops found in other cities like Rome, Alexandria presented a charismatic and academic tradition. The Christian Platonists of Alexandria hold an undisputed place in the history and thought of Christianity as the first intellectuals to try constructing a Christian philosophy.[1]

While the founder and first master of the Alexandrian School was Pantainos, it is his successor, Clement of Alexandria who is best known. Clement gladly accepted the best gifts of non-Christian philosophy as providing pointers towards Christ, who is the Truth *par excellence.* This thinker, always so optimistic about the possibilities of the human intellect, was also uncompromising in his teaching about God's otherness or transcendence:

Though heaven be called his throne, yet he is not contained, even while resting delighted in his creation.[2]

The picture of this cosmic hierarchy is a great living chain through which each link attracts those below in response to the overpowering attraction of the divine beauty.[3]

Clement's humanism is proof of his positive attitude toward creation: his reference to divine beauty, the importance that he attaches to using worldly pleasures properly. Yet Clement's *gnostic,* as he calls the person who reaches perfection, enjoys worldly pleasures in a spirit of detachment, because these are ultimately irrelevant to salvation. The view that material goods can be enjoyed simply because they are in themselves insignificant might be considered the backbone of capitalistic consumerism. Clement's *gnostic* uses but does not actively transform the material world. The *gnostic* may in many ways be an admirable figure, but what is absent is any sign of struggle or stress for the transfiguration of the world. Thus, in reality, Clement is far less a humanist than the more rigorist or ascetic Christian writers. For him, *truth... is always a homeless stranger in the historical order.*[4] For Christianity, however, Truth assumed flesh and found a home in Bethlehem, in Nazareth, and on Golgotha.

ORIGEN (c.185-254)–THE DEPTH OF THE WORLD

With Origen, who was Clement's successor as head of the School, we may begin to discuss specifically Christian mysticism.[5] He was neither a convert from philosophy like Clement before him, nor a philosopher like Plotinus after him. Origen was concerned with interpreting Scripture, which he saw as the repository of all truth, and which lies at the heart of his mystical theology and of his life's work. Origen is two-sided, however: there is the traditional, ecclesiastical side; and there is also the Platonist, speculative side. This great representative of Alexandrian Christianity reveals a far more subtle and differentiated scheme than his predecessor Clement, although one which ultimately undergoes very similar difficulties.

From both Greek philosophy and Scripture, Origen inherits the conviction that God is unknowable; yet Origen is reluctant to entertain the notion of God's radical unknowability. His is a mysticism of light, not of darkness, where the summit of mystical experience is knowledge and illumination. To know the light of Christ is our highest privilege as fleshly beings. But we are not just flesh, and so Christian maturity involves a progressive detachment from the *fleshly Jesus* who must give way to the spiritual or *interior gospel.* Origen is scandalized by flesh and matter, and he is clearly embarrassed by the scene at Gethsemane.[6] For him the goal of the mystic is knowledge of the Word of God prior to and independent of the Incarnation. The soul passes beyond faith in the Incarnation, which constitutes simply a preliminary stage in its ascent to God.

Likewise, for Origen, natural contemplation primarily signifies not so much the contemplation of the wonder of God in creation, but a perception of the transience of this world and a desire to move beyond it:

The human mind should mount to spiritual understanding, and seek the ground of things in heaven.[7]

By the same token, Origen sees ethics as that which subdues the body to the soul and, in the final resort, frees the soul from bondage to the material body.

Origen's attitudes to the material world and to historical reality remain problematic, and there is ultimately a tension between the biblical theologian and the philosophical speculator. While he never explicitly claims that matter and history are insignificant, no doubt he considers them an imperfection and a distortion of what is truly human. God is of course to be encountered in the world, although the form of the encounter is only a *shadow.*

While the influence and inheritance of Platonist thought is evident in the works of Origen, there is no evidence that he outrightly devalues the material world. After all, if one believes material things to be an image of heavenly reality, how can one despise them? The weakness of Platonism lies rather in its lack of historical compassion and concern; its world is largely static. Origen, however, speaks of *moving forward, never stopping,*[8] thereby succeeding in giving to history a story and to matter a place within the cosmos.

The question still remains whether Origen's Christ is less than fully incarnate, whether his Christ has–in colloquial terms–fully *made touch-down.* Ultimately, Origen is unwilling to confront and embrace human life and material creation, though he was a brilliant and elusive thinker, and the precursor of more than one aspect of the Christian mystical tradition. Although later theology developed different emphases, these were nonetheless formed within the fundamental framework provided by this great Alexandrian thinker.

PLOTINUS (204-270)–THE SOUL OF THE WORLD

Perhaps the greatest philosopher of religion in the ancient world, Plotinus was taught by Ammonius Sakkas, the renowned teacher of the school in Alexandria, but did not start writing until age 50. Towards the middle of the third century, Plotinus opened his own school in Rome.

Plotinus is known as the most prominent representative of *neoplatonist* philosophy. His school of Neoplatonism did not just modify or revise Platonism, but drew from the entire classical tradition to produce a new synthesis.[9]

Despite seeing the cosmos as a hierarchy wherein the heavenly bodies, including the sun and the stars, are recognized as spiritual bodies, Plotinus adopted a seemingly negative attitude towards matter. For Plotinus, matter is without form or shape, a nothing, almost like the chaos out of which creation came. Even so, Plotinus evidently sought to oppose the Gnostics of his time who saw the material world as being evil or inferior. He claimed that no one could look upon the world and deduce that its origin lay in some demonic power. Salvation then should not be identified with any escape from matter.

In spite, then, of its rational and spiritual basis, ancient Greek philosophy ultimately achieved a certain balance between spirit and matter, always preserving a sense of awe and wonder before creation. This appears to be the case in both Platonist and Aristotelian thought. Indeed, these two philosophical currents serve in this way to complement one another, thereby avoiding the extremes of idealism and materialism.

There exists in Plotinus the basis for a concept of theism or even what we know as process theology. Some critics though deny that, and prefer to call Plotinus a pantheist. Admittedly, there are passages in Plotinus that support the supremacy of God over the world, as well as passages that undermine any distinction between God and the world. One could move in either direction, since Plotinus has a strong sense of both the otherness and the affinity of God with the world. His dialectical philosophy considers creation as a world of opposites.

At the same time, Plotinus' world tends towards (universe) and expresses a sense of oneness (uni-ty). The cosmos reveals order and organization, identity and repetition. Logic demands repetition, for things must *come back* in order for a unity to be recognized in the diversity. This multiplicity exists within ourselves, as well, though Plotinus ascribes priority and preference to unity. Strictly speaking, in the end Plotinus does not have a doctrine of creation, at least in the way that Christian theology would assert this doctrine. The *One* brings forth everything by a kind of overflow or emanation of its divine being. This kind of language is common to the Wisdom literature of the Old Testament, but the biblical emphasis on God's transcendence is lacking. So let us consider some biblical terms here. *Barra* is the word for creation by God, while the vaguer term *assa* refers to the making of the lesser stars or the products of human beings. The artist, for example, may create a work of art but the result is also an extension or emanation of the artist. So perhaps the Bible, though stressing creation, does not entirely exclude emanation. After all, is it not the idea of a de-divinized cosmos that is the cause of our lack of feeling and dignity for the earth upon which we tread? The emanationist model of creation was formally rejected by the Church; yet the classical Christian writers retained some of its overtones, such as the presence of the one God in all things and in all people (cf. Gen. 1:26).

The *One*, therefore, seeks communion of its being, that which overflows and emanates, and that which is fulfilled by returning to its creator. The mind is able to grasp things in their unity, holding together the indissoluble union of thought and matter.

Furthermore, there is a *soul* that also embraces the body of the world, and each soul belongs to the one cosmic soul. When one soul suffers, so does another, and so does the world soul, while at the same time each soul does not lose its individuality. There are even grades or degrees of soul-ness. And God, who is beyond all souls, personally shares in the suffering of the world.

DIONYSIUS THE AREOPAGITE (5TH-6TH centuries) –THE DIVERSITY OF THE WORLD

Highly esteemed in both eastern and western Christianity, the writings of Dionysius are first mentioned early in the sixth century. Although the authenticity of his writing was challenged almost from the very outset, it is only in this century that serious doubts actually arose. The perpetrator also of much historical confusion, the author of these various works is not the disciple of the Apostle Paul, mentioned in the Book of Acts, but in fact the most faithful disciple of Plotinus in the Christian tradition. Dionysius probably flourished around the year 500, and may well have been of Syriac origin. Of all ancient writers, he attempted the most complete synthesis of the neoplatonist and the biblical traditions, of the Hellenistic and the Hebrew world views.

In contrast to Plotinus who, as we have seen, felt that higher beings *create* lower ones through emanation, Dionysius believed that the higher level transmits life to those below. Despite the politically incorrect overtones of the term *hierarchy,* there is no denying the gradations in the universe itself: animals, vegetables, molecules, atoms, and so on. Leaving anthropocentrism behind does not necessarily mean a move towards indiscriminate *egalitarianism.* In Christ's own words, there is a definite hierarchy of values:

Are you [human beings] not of more value than they [the birds of the air?] (Matt. 6:26)

In the Dionysian hierarchy, the higher order is responsible for charging meaning and life into the lower order, with the latter never undermined or trivialized by the former. Both contribute to the richness and beauty of divine life. It is what we might today call *bio-diversity.* There is a dynamism in this view of reality, which envisages reciprocal relations between the levels of being and is aware of the inward relations of outward things.

Nonetheless, there is also an undeniable emphasis on the transcendence of God, who is not only at the peak of the scale, but above and beyond it. God's being is the very being of all that exists. Like Plotinus, Dionysius is accused of overemphasizing transcendence to the point of pantheism. Yet Dionysius also states that God, out of divine love *(eros)* for creation, moves outside of the divine nature in an act of ecstatic self-emptying *(kenosis)* towards the world:

The creator of all...moves outside of himself in an act of extreme erotic love...[and approaches the world] burning with great goodness and love and eros.[10]

God, so to speak, *crosses the threshold* (Teilhard de Chardin) of divine nature in relating to creation. Dionysian cosmology and anthropology include motion; perfection is not static but involves transfiguration. At this point, the Dionysian ecstasy introduces a dynamic note into the understanding of the relationship between God and the world. Neoplatonist and Christian elements come together in an active transcendence of a living and loving God, who is neither static nor aloof. And here Dionysius becomes the archetypal theologian of the di-polar God that is found in contemporary process theology:[11] a God beyond all being, whose nature it is to be self-emptied. This act of loving self-humiliation or kenosis is an essential, and not just an exceptional dimension of God (cf. Phil. 2:7-8).

JOHN SCOTUS ERIUGENA (c.810-877) –THE UNIVERSALITY OF THE WORLD

In ninth-century Ireland, Scotland and Wales, monasteries preserved theological thought alive. It was there that John Scotus Eriugena received his education before going to France where he taught philosophy. With his knowledge of Greek, he was able to translate the writings of Dionysius into Latin. During his life, he was not popular: his students murdered him, and the Western Church condemned his writings in 1210. Recently, however, there has been renewed interest in his works and he is even regarded as a forerunner of some modern religious thought.

Eriugena's language is similar to that of Dionysius and Plotinus. Though none of them should be written off as pantheists, the term is more appropriate in Eriugena's case. Eriugena speaks of a *universal nature,* a universe that consists of all nature, including God and the creatures. God, however, is not identified with the whole of nature but only with the part which *creates and is not created.* Creating is the defining characteristic of God; God is not merely a part of it but also lies apart from it. Eriugena tries to hold together divine transcendence and divine immanence without undermining either. Impossible to express consistently, Eriugena resorts to paradoxical language:

God and the world are not two separate realities but belong together in a single whole. God is all things everywhere; he is never cut off from his creation anywhere.

Eriugena carefully preserves the otherness of God, that God is the creator or cause of all things; hence, one may readily affirm his existence. Yet there is a new logic that must be applied when referring to God: if one attributes a particular property to God, then one must also predicate its opposite. For what is for us normally a contradiction is in fact a reality when speaking of God. This is what Nicholas of Cusa (see the paragraph below) will, in the fifteenth century, call the *coincidence of opposites.* Nothing can be said properly of God, because God transcends all understanding. Yet from the order of things God may be seen to be wise, or more than *(plusquam)* wise. From the very motion of the world, God is seen to be its life.

God is not defined but the One who defines. God is *motion at rest* and *rest in motion,* while all things move from God and to God. However, there is sufficient *reflection* of God in creation to permit speaking metaphorically of him. God, therefore, is not estranged from the world; but Eriugena goes one step further–every visible and invisible creature can, at least potentially, be called a revelation of God, a theophany. Where, at the beginning of the Christian era, Philo the Alexandrian Jew referred to God as leaving traces of himself in his works, Eriugena advances this notion and speaks of the very works of God as constituting divine verity, in effect being a mode of divine existence.

This idea of the *consequent nature* of God is expounded by contemporary process theologians, though Eriugena is considered more a philosopher than a theologian. Perhaps this is why he does not seriously consider the reality of evil and sin, and why his writings bear the imprint of gnosticism and less the weight of traditional incarnational theology.

NICHOLAS OF CUSA (1401-1464) –COSMIC SYNTHESIS

Nicholas of Cusa claims to have come across the writings of Dionysius only after his own mystical illumination, but he is certainly very much indebted to his Eastern predecessor. In his works, there is a sharpening of the traditional dialectical language about God.

Nicholas, a mathematician, was fascinated by the concept of infinity. For Nicholas, God contains and transcends all conflicts and contradictions. God is the *coincidence* or *concordance of opposites,* because the divinity embraces everything, even differences and diversities. All dichotomies and divisions are somehow synthesized in God who is the interconnection of all consciousness. We can only wonder at how great God is. Nicholas claims that the more learned one is, the more ignorant one realizes that one is.[12] This echoes Dionysius for whom knowledge is being blinded by an excess of light. This *blindness* or *blissfullness* is the experience of unity, whereby we are aware that separation is but an illusion. Similar notions may be found in Athanasius of Alexandria, who discerns a sense of concord even in the apparent discord of the world:

A pure and simple realization: beings of opposite natures can unite in a concord of harmony. There is a harmony, for instance, among the seasons: spring follows winter, summer follows spring, and autumn follows summer... It is impossible not to realize that there must be a superior being...that gives unity to their multiplicity, and orders their existence... In the universe there is no disorder, only order; no disharmony, only concord...[13]

Nevertheless, God is absolute, the reason for all things. Everything exists and subsists in God, who is the absolute *quiddity* (or *thing-ness)* of the world. God penetrates all: he is the center of all, as well as the circumference of all in eluding differences. In his later work *The Vision of God,*[14] Nicholas' image of the omnivoyant face whose eyes follow us everywhere attempts to combine the polarities of God's universality (which does not swallow up time and particularity) and God's concreteness (which is not swallowed up by eternity and infinity). Nicholas writes of the *face of all faces* which is beheld in every face. The absolute face of God is discovered over the entire face of the world.

Despite his attempts to *personify* the God of his philosophy, Nicholas of Cusa is usually criticized for the validity of mathematical examples that he adopts in his writings. But he has made theological truth of his mathematical speculation. It was the negative or apophatic theology of the Eastern tradition which safeguarded, it seems, for that tradition the transcendence of the living God who alone is worshiped. It was this theology which assisted Eastern writers in avoiding the absolutization of any concept or term.

THE DISTINCTION BETWEEN ESSENCE AND ENERGIES

Scripture and the Eastern Christian classics do not divide grace and nature or spirit and matter. The fundamental dichotomy in Judaeo-Christian literature is not between nature and grace, but rather between two levels within human nature–the fallen and the unfallen, the sinful and the redeemed. Created nature is the only premise and promise for salvation or destruction; it is not a finished product, but a moving ground in a process of continuous self-transcendence and transformation.

Contemporary Western theology no longer espouses God as eternal substance, a concept proposed by classical Greek philosophy and characteristic of medieval scholasticism. The Eastern Christian tradition modified this Hellenistic concept of God as immobile essence, though not to the point of embracing the opposite, a God who is conceived of as becoming. A systematic examination of the notion of God in Scripture, liturgy, and spirituality reveals a God who moves between these two poles.

In its attempt to reconcile the *immutability* or *stability* of God with his *becoming* or *historicity,* i.e. his involvement in human hearts and history, Eastern theology is inevitably directed towards the "difference-unity" model. Tracing back at least as far as the fourteenth century with Gregory Palamas, this model relates the immutable essence to the uncreated energies of God. The latter manifest the infinite possibilities of the inexhaustible richness in the former, as well as the acts which express these possibilities. The energies of God–what the Hebrew Scriptures refer to as God's glory *(kabod)*–charge the created world with reality and transparency, allowing it to reveal and conceal the mystery of God. The Christian God transcends all opposition and contradiction; God dwells in the dialectic of grace and in the paradox of love.

This distinction between divine essence and divine energies defines the relationship between God and creation. In other words, nothing is outside the embrace of God. Everything is directly related to God and dependent upon God, inasmuch as it is a reflection of the divinity. At the same time, God's essence remains totally transcendent and undetermined. This paradox is prescribed and preserved in the Orthodox teaching of St. Gregory Palamas but already apparent in the earlier Christian tradition.[15] Thus Palamas writes:

On the one hand, the divine super-essentiality is never called multiple; on the other hand, the divine and uncreated grace and energy of God is, being indivisibly divided, like the sun's ray, which warms and lightens and vivifies and increases its own splendor in what it enlightens, and shines forth in the eyes of the beholders; in the way, then, of this faint image the divine energy of God is called not one, but multiple, by the theologians; and thus Basil the Great declares: "What are the energies of the Spirit? Their extent cannot be told, and they are numberless. How can we comprehend what is beyond the ages? What are the energies of that which precedes the intelligible creation?" For before the intelligible creation and prior to the ages (for the ages themselves are intelligible creations), no one has ever said, or considered, that there is anything created. Therefore, the powers and energies of the divine Spirit, which are, according to the theologians, multiple, are uncreated, indivisibly distinguished from the entire Essence of the undivided Spirit.[16]

The paradox of divine transcendence and divine immanence was succinctly stated in recent years by Philip Sherrard:

For if only the total transcendence of God is affirmed, then all created things, all that is in change and visible, must be regarded as without any real roots in the Divine, and hence as entirely negative and 'illusory' in character; while if only the total immanence of God is affirmed, then creation must be looked upon as real in its own right, instead of as real only because it derives from and participates in the Divine; and the result must be a pantheism, and a worship of creation rather than of the Creator, which must ultimately lead to the notion that God is superfluous, and hence to an entirely materialistic conception of things. The full Christian understanding demands, thus, the simultaneous recognition of both the total transcendence and the total immanence of the Divine, the affirmation of the one at the expense of the other being the negation of this understanding and the supreme doctrinal error; and it was for this recognition that Christian theologians had to find an adequate doctrinal expression.[17]

GOD AND THE WORLD

The universe is never totally external to God but is in God, Yet the limitations of such terms must be acknowledged. On the other hand, the essence-energies distinction allows for the transcendence of God as well as for divine free-willed activity in the world.

Process theologians have made moves toward the essence-energies doctrine in their distinction between the primordial and consequent nature of God. In response,

Orthodox theologians would say that the personal distinction of the Trinity in God should not be undermined, while the distinction between the primordial and consequent sides in God must not be merely a philosophical exercise. For the Orthodox, the essence-energies distinction remains real at all times, even in regard to the state of deification and the life beyond. Process theology has in recent years revived the concept of *panentheism,* i.e. that God includes or incorporates the world, while not being exhausted or effaced by the world. The inherent danger there is that God, being almost identified with creation, may cease to evoke a sense of adoration and wonder.

The Orthodox doctrine of the divine essence and the divine energies has much to offer in an age when the relationship or reconciliation between God and the cosmos must be affirmed. The essence-energies distinction takes seriously both the human responsibility for the whole of creation, as well as the divine redemption and transfiguration of the whole world.

The God contemplated by the Christian mystics in the middle ages was a God elusive yet familiar, both transcendent and immanent; it was a God *afar* and at the same time *at hand* (Jer. 22:23). This is the God that is worshiped in heaven, and venerated on earth. In the chapters that follow, we shall discover how this God is celebrated in the Eastern tradition, and especially in the ascetic tradition of the desert.

CHAPTER FIVE

The Sacredness of Creation in *The Sayings of the Desert Fathers*

THE WORLD OF THE "SAYINGS"

The paradox of divine transcendence and divine immanence is evident not only in the intellectual tradition, but also in the unwritten and unlettered wisdom of the desert. It is to this more practical *school* that we shall now turn our attention. Ascetic writers of earlier centuries, the desert Fathers and Mothers and their successors, pursued rigorously the complicated issues of the divine Incarnation, precisely because they concretely experienced this *double aspect* as a powerful symbol of the union within themselves of body and soul. For life in the desert revealed the inextricable interdependence of body and soul, as well as the total identification of Christ with the world. God, human nature, and the world were generally appreciated and approached in terms of real sharing. In the world of *The Sayings of the Desert Fathers,* the purely ascetic is raised to the level of mysticism. The way that these desert dwellers related to their environment reflects the worship that they reserved for their God.

The *Sayings of the Desert Fathers* grew out of the experience of fourth-century asceticism in Egypt, Syria and Palestine. Originally an oral and fluid tradition, remembered and circulated among the monks themselves, its written form evades precise dating; it is as rough and craggy as the desert landscape that surrounded these hermits, precluding any systematization. Even so, these *apophthegmata* transmit the beauty of creation, and all the wit and witness of the desert.[1] Here Moses encountered God, Elijah heard God, Anthony spoke to God, and John Climacus recorded his ascent to God. These proverbs are an ascetic parallel to doctrinal and conciliar formulations. But the way of the desert dwellers is that of humility, of action in *silence*, unlike some of the ostentatious and *loud* actions in the Church.

There is in the desert a symbolic defiance, a revelation of the supremacy of the Spirit above all institutions and gender. And though the ascetic collection includes the words of only three women–among one hundred and twenty seven men–we need to remember that only recently has the sin of patriarchy been called to question.

LOVE OF THE LAND

The world which the desert Fathers and Mothers inhabited was a barren and threatening terrain, a place of temptation and transfiguration alike. The flight of these monks into uninhabitable regions was as much revolutionary as a natural outpouring of the life of the church. From the earliest Scriptural image, creation is presented as food to a human being who is hungry, ultimately of God. *The earth and its fullness* (Psalm

23:1) must be transformed into living flesh and blood, the desert grains into human cells. Any other concept of the land reduces the created order to a purely secular or utilitarian function, even to communion with death. The desert is to be refashioned and re-created, because the grace of God and the struggle of the ascetic renders the unredeemed wasteland into a purgative preparation for salvation.

Thus, when Anthony was brought to the *interior mountain,* he is said to have seen the place and loved it.[2] This admiration and awe for the land is characteristic of early monasticism. Within the existing records, one observes a dichotomy: the desert is the horrifying prospect and the ugly perspective of the demonic, while at the same time inviting and inciting the hermit to move further and deeper into the unknown and deserted. The monastic sets out on the long, arid road of spirituality with a view to attaining love's countenance. It is the coupling of treading through the created order, the proof of God's immanence, in order to reach the Creator in his transcendence. Thus the personal pursuit and crucial criterion contain a paradox: the conviction that one single vivid experience of this desirous love in all its intensity will advance one much further than the most arduous struggle against the passions and the severest ascetic enterprise. It is the propelling forward in love to God which allows the ascetic to put aside desires of the flesh and accounts for the otherwise unaccountably extreme and apparently senseless feats. The true home of the ascetics has at all times been the desert, and so

Church and desert are almost understood as one. No wonder that early Christian literature admits no sharp contrast between the Church in the world and the spirituality of the saint isolated in a remote place or perched on a pillar.

The desert is not just some eccentric calling. Rather, it is the center of creation, the crux of matter and of what matters in the world. The awareness of oneness with the past–whether with the prophets or forbears in general–inspires a keen sense of continuity and communion, rendering this tradition alive. And there is the recognition of kinship with the land, communion on both a personal and a cultural plane.

Through the desert, the ascetics believe that they are in profound personal communion with God. This intense feeling of solidarity with both the historical and the eternal, of consistency between heaven and earth, renders the desert a point of mediation between created and Creator, and the humble inhabitant of the desert at once *microcosm* and *microtheos*. The dream of a restored creation is the ultimate vision in the desert, where everything that is not whole and holy is but diabolical illusion. And in the desert the demons are as countless as the grains of sand. The desert is the perfect symbol for God and creation–outwardly barren, ineffable even, but inwardly teeming.

In their *remoteness* from the world, the inhabitants of the desert present us with a world-view that is neither anti-cosmic nor a-cosmic. Their asceticism is not closed to the sacred nature of aesthetical beauty. Their spirituality is neither escapist from nor hostile to sensible and earthly things. In brief, the genuine desert dweller is far removed from the dualism that has often been fostered in intellectual monastic circles throughout the centuries and that has, at least theoretically (and sometimes officially) been condemned by the Christian Church, though it always perilously tempts its practitioners. The desert Fathers and Mothers are convinced that not only are we to respect and care for the land but that, in the mutual relationship and solidarity with the whole of creation, the earth too cares for us–long before it actually covers us. This is why remembrance of death is so important for the desert ascetic:

Abba Cassian related about an old man who said: "When I am dead, plant my stick in the grave; if it grows and bears fruit, know that I am pure... But if it does not grow, know that I have sinned." So they planted the stick and on the third day it budded and bore fruit, and they all gave glory to God.[3]

LIFE IN THE LAND

The desert culture is based on movement, and, at least in the writings of the more erudite mystics, on the flight from the body[4] and its desire for material possessions.[5] In the desert the body sweats, toils, expands; one is estranged not only from creation but also from one's self. But desert asceticism presents a curious ambivalence–the body is not simply decorative but substantive, not just attractive but essential. Still, there exists a temptation to regard created matter as evil. Though hints of this attitude appear in desert literature, the central teaching is free of it, even in the extremest of ascetic practices. For example, despite the harsh discipline, Anthony's body is in better condition than prior to its twenty years of solitude:

The picture that is given us of Anthony, as he emerged from his solitude, is in no way of an ascetic emaciated by asceticism that is its own end: it is of a man calmed, brought into equilibrium, in whom everything human has become, as it were, transparent to the Spirit, docile to his influence.[6]

One might even say that Anthony was attuned to and *in equilibrium* with the whole of his environment, indicating the ascetics' yearning for an equitable society and a restored creation.

Flight to the desert should not be confused with a need to move somewhere else. In fact, Anthony's advice is for the need to *stay in one's cell.*[7] Thus, the exodus into the desert is less a movement away from than a movement into the realm where one encounters God. In the cell, the hermit faces the most grueling temptations, in addition to the most intimate relations with God. There one contemplates the world as a revelation of God's beauty. In contemplating nature, the hermit becomes aware of things divine and of the world as a revelation of God's beauty. The sacrifice of renunciation means little unless there is, first, a true esteem of the world as created by God. If sin is considered the failure to accept and assume the world as a gift from God, then denial of the gift of beauty cannot be considered sacrifice or sacred. Therefore, asceticism essentially affirms, rather than denies the fullness of life and the beauty of the world. The desert Fathers and Mothers do not provide us with a set of feats or facts, but rather present us with a story that affirms the whole of creation. The greatest achievement of the desert Fathers and Mothers was the transformation that they wrought upon the world around them. Ascetic struggle betrays the authentic hermit not as hard, but as intensely loving, recognizing in creation the unique *icon* of divinity. Abba Anthony said:

Renounce this life, so that you may be alive to God.[8]

Therefore, movement in the desert culture entails plunging ahead as pilgrims–in spite of the thorns and sharp stones of the desert–forward and upward into deeper and ever-deepening levels of self-knowledge and of divine vision.

A significant dimension of desert spirituality is its apophatic or negative nature. The intense heat and flat barrenness of the desert seem to lead nowhere. The vast emptiness and desolate vacancy uncover another peculiar, yet refreshing aspect of the desert, namely its imageless silence. No matter how divine the image discovered in solitude may be, the desert nevertheless demands that the hermit moves beyond this and all other images. The process of *stripping* or *letting go* is necessary to relate properly to one's God, one's world and oneself. It is essential in order to realize that in God (the transcendent) alone we discover our world (the immanent) and our true selves (self-transcendence). The intellect needs the chastening stillness of the desert. *Detachment* means traveling light–and one can often manage with much less than imagined; it also implies traveling without stopping–continual movement forward and upward. In the desert, there can be no *defense mechanisms,* no *toys for distraction.* One must look within and face directly the pain and passion of life in all its intensity. As the well-known "Twelve Step" programs put it: *No pain, no gain.* And Anthony of Egypt experienced this in the fourth-century desert:

Whoever has not experienced temptation cannot enter the kingdom of heaven... Without temptations no one is saved.[9]

This apophatic element is fostered in the desert tradition, where the monk is *denuded of all things,*[10] at all times a beginner.[11] Retreating into the desert makes allowance for the boundless grace of God. The *apophasis* of distance and silence provokes the unconditional action of God. And the revelation of God imposes the required silence in order to listen to and love God.

GOD AND THE LAND

The desert's sacramental dimension, its sacredness, lies in its stark, abased remoteness. Standing as a sign and safeguard of authenticity, the desert is prized because it is inaccessible, ultimately unendangered by any outside interference. Thus it reflects–crudely and austerely, but most immediately–a direct encounter with nature and God. There are no frills, no comfort–little wonder then that *simplicity* and *forthrightness* are singled out as virtues in both manual labor *(labora)* and prayer *(ora)*. The desert Fathers and Mothers bow reverently before the sacredness of the surrounding land, cooperating and identifying with the earth, and convinced that both humanity and earth belong to heaven, that the contract between heaven and earth (cf. Isaiah 24:4-7) must be renewed. There is, among them, an uncompromising recognition that every minute particle of the created world is solely and totally God's. The monks are called to cultivate the desert (cf. Isaiah 35:1) because God speaks not just through the desert dwellers but also through creation itself.[12]

Hence the desert Fathers and Mothers live in harmony with wild beasts (cf. III Kings 17:6, Jonah 2, Daniel 6) and the entire animal kingdom, over which they enjoy the loving authority of God.[13] This attitude of care and preservation is also extended toward the *elements* of creation[14] which are profoundly respected and *admired*, though not *adored*.[15] By the Incarnation, creation is filled with the presence of God: *Everything is sanctified through his presence*, writes the Great Elder, Barsanuphius, in his *Letters* which expound in detail the elusive glimpses offered by the *Sayings*.[16] In some *supernatural* way, creation itself protects the monks, too.

So the desert ascetic seeks to safeguard the purity of the land which he has received from earlier generations. Creation, too, forms a central part of this tradition:

Children, let us not pollute this place, which has been cleansed by our Fathers.[17]

NEW HEAVEN AND NEW EARTH

Be joyful at all times, exclaims Abba Benjamin.[18] Beyond any emphasis on ascetic feats or individual sinfulness, the ulterior message of the Desert Fathers and Mothers is one of pervasive light and inexpressible joy. Indeed, their charming humor portrays less a sense of escapism than an expression of humility, reducing the tension between nature and grace, clay and fire, creation and Creator. The light and joy of the *other* world spill over and penetrate *this* world.

The language [of the desert ascetics] is alien to contemporary culture. Yet, we need to re-examine and re-express their ideals because in their essential nature, they articulate not ascetic feats for the spiritually agile but aesthetic aspirations that transcend time and culture. They embrace values which seem to be eminently appropriate for the holistic vision of life.[19]

If you will, you can become all flame, cries Joseph of Panepho.[20] By enflaming their very selves, these ascetics betray the flame of God's energies that consumes all creation. By rendering transparent the treasure in their *earthen vessel* (II Cor. 4:7), the desert elders illumine the density of *the vase of the desert.*[21] In the image of God or *theophany* that they incur, a real transparency or *diaphany* occurs, and beyond the shattered world the mysterious presence of the living God is gradually discerned. By imploring, in the seclusion of the desert, for the restoration of the whole polluted cosmos, they establish *a new heaven and a new earth* (Rev. 21:1).

CHAPTER SIX

The Desert is Alive

Having withdrawn into the desert, abba Arsenius prayed to God: "Lord, lead me in the way of salvation." And he heard a voice saying: "Arsenius, flee, be silent, pray always."[1]

THE MYTH OF THE DESERT

In many ways, the early period of the Desert Fathers and Mothers–the fourth and fifth centuries–resembles current times: a separated, even opposed Church and State; imminent moral and economic collapse; apparent political and social upheaval; the rise of secularism. The Church itself could easily be criticized for compromising, for no longer being convincing. There was, in brief, a very real crisis of confidence and security both from within and without.

It is hard to imagine imitating the behavior and ideals of the early Desert Fathers and Mothers, though one can discover in these occasionally eccentric ascetics a genuine source of inspiration. It is perhaps more appropriate to refer to the myth of the desert as a way of life that entails a symbolic depth, an inner meaning, and a secret or sacrament that must be explored.

The collection of the desert elders' *sayings* comprises

neither accounts of their life nor records of their teaching, but glimpses of the fire and light that inspired them, life-giving words of salvation offered by an elder to spiritual children. Apart from the influence of the New Testament, it is the Desert Fathers who had the most profound and far-reaching effect on the spiritual development of both Eastern and Western Christendom.

The following pages will examine the fundamental virtues extolled in the desert experience as gleaned from the revelation to Arsenius quoted at the beginning of this chapter. The purpose is to discern the way in which the desert elders were able to live in a harmonious relationship with their neighbor and with their land, that is to say with their immediate environment. Therefore, in referring here to the desert, I am alluding to the flight to the desert (as the movement to a particular place), the silence of the desert (as the movement within one's heart), and the notion of continual prayer (as the movement toward God).

The desert is a powerful image that cannot be lightly dismissed inasmuch as it constitutes a stage through which the soul is required to pass, both individually and collectively.[2]

Unfortunately we have today either romanticized or else resisted the notion of the desert:

Apparently with the rise of industry, we began to romanticize the wilderness–which is to say we began to institutionalize it within the concept of the "scenic." Because of railroads and improved highways, the wilderness was no longer an arduous passage for the traveler, but something to be looked at as grand or beautiful from the high vantages of the roadside. We became viewers of "views." And because we no longer traveled in the wilderness as a matter of course, we forgot that wilderness still circumscribed civilization and persisted in domesticity. We forgot, indeed, that the civilized and the domestic continued to depend upon wilderness, that is, upon natural forces within the climate and within the soil that have never in any meaningful sense been controlled or conquered. Modern civilization has been built largely in this forgetfulness.[3]

People have in fact always preferred to inhabit the *non-desert-like*, the coastal, the marginal areas. Earthy areas are commonly accepted as belonging to the lowly and poor; those more *fortunate* prefer city balconies and elevators. Life in the city is so often an escape from the land to the abstractions of wealth and power. I am not suggesting a return to the desert in the manner of the Recchabites, who in biblical times took to the desert. Rather, I am alluding to a return to the concept of desert as our true place within the world and of recognizing our responsibility for the world. For just as the ruthless urbanization of the countryside and the heedless exploitation of natural resources have cosmic implications for the world today, so also the desert has borne the crucial consequences of our history and spirituality. In the desert experience, one learns, or relearns, what in the Orthodox hymnography is termed *the reality of matter, the truth of things.* The desert came alive in its monastic dwellers of the fourth and fifth centuries, and we should learn from them about our relationship with the earth that we inhabit.

"ARSENIUS, FLEE!"

The desert is described in many ways both in Scripture and in the Christian classics. It is seen as a specific place–an area separated from and deprived of God;[4] a location, outside of the city, where one is exiled and executed like Christ;[5] an area where one confronts and fights the demons;[6] the abomination of desolation;[7] or even more positively, an opportunity for dialogue and communion with God.[8] However, it would possibly be better to picture the desert not so much as a place but above all as a mysterious way[9] that includes all the intensity of a symbol or sacrament. It is the desire for the transcendent that is in itself more desirable than any worldly satisfaction (see Psalm 62:1). The desert speaks in a coarse but realistic manner; its voice may not appear eloquent but it is clearly life-giving, resembling the sound *of many waters* (Ezek. 1:24).

Formal structures and supports crumble; there remains only a veiled God and a promise. The flight to the desert is a search for God in the dryness of daily life, in the tediousness of routine. The flight is less an escape from society and the world, as it is a pressing and powerful attraction towards God,[10] who retires to the heart of the desert. The descent into the heart is more than romantic nostalgia for the boundless or for the abyss of divinity. The nomadic element of those who *wander in deserts, and in mountains, and in dens and caves of the earth* (Hebrews 11:39) reflects the worship of the absolute. The departure from one's own narrow limitations and the resulting spiritual contact with the infinite is a call beyond, an invitation to transfiguration.

Many have gone to the desert, either figuratively or literally. In his account of the monks in Egypt, Rufinus writes:

This is the utter desert where each monk remains alone in his cell... There is a huge silence and a great quiet there.[11]

Yet one is in fact least alone in the desert: Abraham was alone; Moses stood in solitude; and Elijah, too, took the lonely journey to the desert. But because these and others were called to meet and speak to God, they were never less alone than when alone. The inhabitant of the desert, while a *stranger and pilgrim on the earth* (Hebrews 11:13), feels a certain homeliness with God and nature. One reads of the peaceful relationship that monastics have with wild animals,[12] or of the love that ascetics have for the beauty of the wilderness.[13] Recall Isaiah's vision of the peaceful kingdom:

The wolf shall live with the lamb, the leopard shall lie down with the kid, the calf and the lion and the fatling together, and a little child shall lead them. The cow and the bear shall graze, their young shall lie down together; and the lion shall eat straw like the ox. The nursing child shall play over the hole of the asp, and the weaned child shall put its hand on the elder's den. They will not hurt or destroy on all my holy mountain; for the earth will be full of the knowledge of the Lord as the waters cover the sea (Isaiah 11:6-9).

The intense and inner (even innate) desire for God forces the monastic to take to the mountains, somewhere between heaven and earth: Moses' Sinai and Anthony's mountains, Olympus in Asia Minor and the column of the Stylite, Meteora and Athos in Greece. The aim is to ascend the Tabor of the heart. Rather than withdraw from society the monk or nun inevitably creates a new focus of order: they are always alert, *guarding the walls*[14] or frontiers between this life and the next, eagerly expecting the last days and *taking by violence the heavenly kingdom* (Matthew 11:12). The limitations of the desert continually flow and flower into the ultimate grace of God for whom the monk or nun lives, abiding also by the limitations of the desert. This explains the way of life in the desert: the essential content of fasting is to be free to feed on the Word of God without distraction; the inner meaning of silence is to hear this very Word; and the deeper reason for sleeplessness is to expect constantly and earnestly the Bridegroom in the middle of the night (see Matthew 25:1-3).

The desert, however, is also a way of purification, of baptism, and of regeneration.[15] In its almost frightening starkness, it purges the inhabitant from demons, who try to distract and sidetrack one from worship of God in as countless ways as the grains of sand. The monastics are required to beware: the desert itself must not turn into an idol. It is an icon, a unique revelation of God's Word, an infinite source of God's love, but must never become a source of individual pleasure and satisfaction for the sake of deprivation. Asceticism is never aimed at undermining oneself or demeaning the world. It should be a rigor and a discipline worthy of the land and upholding one's own worth.

"BE SILENT"

The desert, says John Chrysostom, *is the mother of quietude.*[16] Silence is a way of interiority, the willingness to explore the center of life, the heart. To possess life to the full (see John 10:10), and encounter life, freedom and love, one must surrender to God and to the world. Where this happens is the desert. There, silence and death go hand in hand; to be utterly silent can feel like death. Sitting in one's cell may be likened to lying in the grave. Yet this is ultimately a healing and comforting experience.

REPENTANCE AND LIFE

The absurd and the intolerable are elements of the desert, and so the issue of hope becomes of vital significance.

Death and the fight for survival introduce a dimension of objectivization and violence in human relations. One must kill in order to live. This absurdity of death in the context of hope is a critical dimension of the desert. Hence, the eucharist is mentioned frequently in desert literature,[17] and indeed the eucharistic approach is evident in loving surrender, in the vulnerability that gives of one's own and one's very self *for the life of the world* (see John 6:51). It is not a way of taking life for survival, but the constant reaffirmation of the words *take, eat, this is my body; take, drink of this my blood* (see Mark 14:22-24).

As in the liturgy, what precedes the Eucharist is repentance (*metanoia*), a complete turn from the cultivation of the ego, and an eradication of the self-will. The desert ascetic does this in an act of abandonment before the cross of Christ. What follows this abandonment in the cross of Eucharist is the resurrection. And so, ultimately, the desert dwellers emphasize not so much their own ugliness but the perfection and beauty of God; the emphasis is not on their own unworthiness but on the treasure in heaven which is given freely. This accounts for the repeated images in the desert literature of light and life, of joy and angels. These ascetics are not gloomy and obsessed, but accessible and very much alive: John of Lycopolis is described as having *a bright and smiling face,* despite years of ascetic feats; Didymus is said to possess *a charming countenance,* despite his unappealing habit of treading on scorpions with bare feet.

The desert monk:

literally overflows. That is an expression which gives some idea of the truth about him. He has a treasure of inexpressible joy hidden in an earthen vessel, small and fragile. And this joy overflows and spreads all around him, filling his surroundings with its fragrance. Light shines from his being. His inner rejoicing sometimes goes beyond his endurance, breaks his heart, shows itself in tears and cries and gestures. And whether he speaks or whether he is silent, whether he sleeps or whether he is awake, whether he is present or whether he is absent, it is always the same thing that he says, the same thing that he is, the same grace and the same power. His presence or the memory of him, the feeling that he is near, or simply that he exists [or that he once existed], of itself conveys something other, something uncreated, tranquil, penetrating. It is something which renews man, calms his nerves, extinguishes his anger, enlightens his mind, gives wings to his hope and prepares him for a struggle that gives quiet and peace to a whole people.[18]

As fantastic as it may seem, humor characterizes the Desert Fathers.[19] Adapted to suit the circumstances at hand, these ascetics take themselves less seriously and concentrate more on God. The humor is by no means a form of escapism but another process of dying, though again in the context of hope; it does not result from despair, cynicism or sarcasm, but serves only to unmask illusion. Humor essentially expresses and identifies humility, reducing the tension between grace and nature, the absolute and relative, fire and clay, God and humanity.

The desert speaks not only to our own mortality, but especially to the mortality of our whole world, and to the transience of our every endeavor that is founded here. In becoming acquainted with the hidden depths of the wilderness, one recognizes that *many are the offspring of the desert* (Isaiah 54:1). Nevertheless, all the great silence merely intensifies and magnifies the singular experience of life. The desert is life (Psalm 77:15 and 19), and there the soul awakens to new life.

HUMILITY AND FREEDOM

Silence underlines the aspect of listening, and it is from this perspective that one needs to consider the obedience and humility of the monk.

The desert transcends the individual; it is far greater than any one human being. The individual must learn to yield to its searing heat: one does not measure it but is measured *by* it. To be isolated in pride is to accept defeat and failure, ultimately to die. It is nature in its most beautiful and its most terrifying. It is the very image of God's own awesome power. One must not only embrace the created world with love and reverence, but submit to and identify with the earth in humility. It is, then, not so much a question of living from but of cooperating with the earth, in the firm conviction that both humanity and the earth belong to heaven. Humanity must renew the contract between heaven and earth, and it can do so only by remaining faithful to the earth. The ground that we tread can no longer be the object of possession, of uncharitable rights,[20] of exploitation. Instead humanity must submit to the dynamism of the land, reverently bowing before the sacredness of place.

The desert schools one in the fundamental realism of humility. But it does not impose itself any more than God does. There is not even the slightest hint of coercion here, whether spiritual or other; only a command. This is why the Desert Fathers and Mothers like to imitate the silence and endurance of the ground. To be humble (*humus* in Latin designates the ground), and to discover the lowliness of the earth, is to be elevated to heaven,[21] because the act *humanizes* nature. Such humility is both theological and ecological, not simply a pious deference or reference to some *spiritual* or other-worldly value. In fact, *the gift of humility is as great as the earth itself*, says Evagrius.[22] The spirit of the desert positively contributes to the theology of failure and sin–precisely because in the end the powerful love of God prevails. The desert experience is that of endurance and fidelity carried out in love, a marriage accepted with the finality of an irrevocable pledge.

The desert dweller is a pauper, a sinner, defined not by the defense of others but by his own personal need, representative of a torn and broken humanity placed before its Savior. These ascetics understand that they are nothing in and by themselves, that they possess nothing that is their *own*. If there is something in them, it is the sense of being loved by God and of belonging to God; their entire life becomes an uncompromising response to this love, a recognition that every minute particle of the world is solely and totally God's. The result is integrity and a lack of pretension, borne out in the silent adoration of God and in their humble veneration of neighbor. In the words of Pachomius:

If you see a person pure and humble, that is a great vision. For what is greater than such a vision, to see the invisible God in a visible human being.[23]

The desert ascetics sought to achieve the ecstasy of tangible love, and this very vision attracted many visitors to their doors.

LEARNING TO LOVE

The desert is as much a school for humility as it is a school of love. For, unlike the contemporary philosophy of *the other person as hell,* the Desert Fathers and Mothers identify their neighbor with God.[24] All too often, though, Christians try to lay upon themselves the moral obligation to love without first realizing the need to understand and to undergo this love slowly and painfully.

Aware of their own limitations, the Desert Fathers and Mothers could show compassion for the weaknesses of others.[25] In their solitude and in their humility, living apart from all, they comprised a part of all. The desert rule was to place hospitality and charity before any rules of fasting and even prayer.[26] Not the great individual fast, nor the feat of endurance, but the principle of love was what counted in the desert:

We should ask of a man not whether devils are subject to him, but whether he possesses love, says the Westerner John Cassian who learned so much from the Egyptian hermits.[27] This love is the ultimate authority of the desert hermit, who is no longer under law but himself passes laws.[28]

The desert elder bows humbly and innocently before humanity and the earth. The result is a merciful–even if at times, in the eyes of the contemporary reader, apparently merciless–perception of the world. It is no wonder that one feels a sense of moral vertigo when reading their words. How can this extreme simplicity and love be reconciled with the extravagance of urban life? Or how might the desert dweller's concern for the transfiguration of the least speck of dust inform the lack of responsibility in social and economic issues? We have already quoted Isaac the Syrian describing the merciful heart. The entire passage portrays:

a heart which is burning with love for the whole of creation, for humans, for birds, for beasts, for demons–for all God's creatures. As he calls them to mind and contemplates them, his eyes fill with tears. From the great and powerful feeling and compassion that grips the

*heart, and from long endurance, his heart diminishes,
and cannot bear to hear or to see any injury or any tiny
sorrow in creation. This is why he constantly offers
prayer with tears for dumb beasts, and for the enemies
of truth, and for those who hurt him, that they may be
protected and shown mercy; likewise he prays for the
race of creeping things, through the great compassion
which fills his heart, immeasurably, after the likeness
of God.*[29]

Confused and confounded by the antithesis of life in but
not of the world, the soul begins to search for salvation
here, on earth, in the very land of desert, and finally falls
in love with the beauty of the world that alone can save
all in all. In this possessing sense of nothingness, of
instability, of insecurity and insufficiency in the desert,
all are plunged: everything, everyone, every possession,
every beauty, every love, every existence.

"PRAY ALWAYS"

Solitude and silence issue in encounter with God through
prayer.[30] External loneliness and wordless quiet are not
sufficient, unless they guide one to inner personal contact
with the One who is the aim of all spiritual and ascetical
struggle. The desert's absence of form and word is a way
of speaking to the Creator in the language of
unpretentious beauty and genuine love, a way of
communication and communion between God and
humanity. The hierarchy in creation is one that reaches
its convergence in God: *all things are yours, and you are
Christ's and Christ is God's* (I Cor. 3:22-23). Belonging

to another world does not undermine, but rather serves to underline the integrity of this world. Distorting our proper focus has mutilated this order: *the land has been infected by its inhabitants; for they have...broken the eternal alliance* (Isaiah 24:4-7). The Desert Fathers and Mothers appear as symbols reminding the Church of its true identity and destiny.

Historians sometimes point out that the early monks avoided taxation and military service by withdrawing to the desert. What they fail to see is that these hermits were primarily conscripted in heaven, paying their dues in blood and tears to the king of heaven and earth. The prologue of the *History of Monks in Egypt* describes them *as loyal children awaiting their father, and as an army expecting its emperor.* They were on the alert, keeping watch for all, paying the dues even of those who had never so much as suspected the need for such a tribute. Indeed, as the author of Hebrews writes, *the world was not worthy of these* (Hebrews 11:38), which is why they took to the desert. The monks pray for those who have no one to pray for them, and for those who do not wish to pray. They are like trees on a busy street, purifying and refreshing through their powerful and prayerful presence.

Confronted with the emptiness, terror, and formlessness of the desert, and in possession of a heart that has become desert, these ascetics had as their ultimate goal *to stand unimpeded in the presence of God.*[31] John the Hermit is said to have stood under a rock *for three years in uninterrupted prayer, not sitting at all or lying down to sleep, but simply snatching some sleep while standing.*[32] Their concern was to discover the vision of God within and through the austerity of the desert, and it is this vision that determined their individual austerities, allowing them to touch reality, to strip away all illusion and to see God.[33] The desert is indeed nothing less than the dwelling-place of God. Just like the clear vision afforded when sand gradually settles in a pool of water, so also is one enabled to view with accuracy and insight both oneself and God.[34] Anthony emerges from the deeper desert, or the *inner mountain* as he calls it, *as from some inmost shrine, initiate into the mysteries and God-borne.*[35]

All asceticism and charity look towards preserving this sacred vision: Anthony seeks to be perfect, Pachomius to do God's perfect will; but both are servants of the glory of God, responsible stewards in the mystery of salvation. The purpose of their contemplation is excentration and concentration upon heaven. Their orientation is towards the light within and beyond this world, and no perspective can diminish this vision of the divinity of this world. This is surely the reason for their seemingly *angelic* state.[36] Yet these hermits remain fully human, realizing the summit of perfection in the depth of humility. The same mystery of the Church is present throughout creation: the Desert Fathers and Mothers see the divine flame in all things, the world as a burning bush of God's energies. In fact their aim is to become fire:

Abba Lot went to see Abba Joseph and said to him, "Abba, as far as I can, I say my little office, I fast a little, I pray and meditate, I live in peace and purity and purify my thoughts. What else can I do?" The old man stood up and stretched his hands towards heaven. His fingers became like ten lamps of fire and he said to him, "If you will, you can become all flame."[37]

This sacred dimension of the human person can only be preserved when the land's integrity also is not mutilated: one is called to the transfiguration of humanity and the world.[38] Only the Church, which underlines the positive aspect of asceticism, constitutes a ray of light and hope. There is a Christian emphasis on fidelity, though it is often restricted to interpersonal relations. But fidelity is the underlying principle of all relations, whether with fellow human beings or with the earth. Any other kind of relationship leads to exploitation and sin, and ultimately to death.

CONCLUSION

The restoration of human nature by Christ's redemption is revealed by such persons as the Desert Fathers and Mothers, who see the entire human race in the context of creation and at home with the whole of creation. There is no sentimental attachment to animals or to nature in the desert, but simply a respectful co-operation and collaboration–even concelebration. It is not surprising that God intervenes *naturally,* by way of miracles or signs that reflect the powerful presence of the divinity. In this sense the desert elders were neither eccentric nor even original, but were in the tradition of the prophets and apostles. They simply sought to live out the inherited road of God in uncharted and voluntary ways.

The desert is not a place of escape but of encounter. People who choose the desert way may seek to preserve silence, but they also protest violently and publicly against the sin of an urbanization which reduces creation to a cycle of production and consumption, and ultimately to destruction. The harshness of the desert comes as provocation: it stands as a searing yet liberating haven between the sterility of a lukewarm religion and the tyranny of fundamentalism; it smashes the perception of prayer and silence as moments of relaxation and individual satisfaction; it pushes aside bourgeois and puritan ideologies that make a connection between virtue and material success; it demands struggle and not mere survival–whether financial, social, emotional, physical or other; it disregards social descent, spiritual class, and native color; it ridicules the frantic pursuit of power and security; it unveils weakness and strives for transcendence. The Desert Fathers and Mothers recognize that the Transcendent is revealed in the most difficult moment of this struggle: God refreshes during the most intense heat of this fire. At the peak of this struggle with God (Genesis 32:24-31), discourse about God becomes (in daring ascetic terminology) intercourse with God. This God is born in barrenness, where there is an absence of pretentiousness and pride; this God fulfills in emptiness, where all space surrenders to and abounds in divine presence.

The desert of the twentieth century is to be found in the world and not in the wilderness, in the city and not in the countryside. It is both a personal pilgrimage, as well as a global aspiration for renewal, reconciliation, and wholeness.

CHAPTER SEVEN

The World of the Icon

THEOLOGY AND MYSTERY

Any discussion of transcendence or transfiguration, at least from an Orthodox perspective, necessarily involves an exploration into the theology and mystery of the icon, that is to say, into the doctrine behind and the vision beyond icons. For the world of the icon not only presupposes a way of thinking and demands a way of living, but also offers new insights into our worldview, new perceptions of the world around us, and something of the eternal in everything we see. Our generation is characterized by a behavior that results from self-centeredness with regard to the natural cosmos: a certain lack of awareness, or recognition, causes us to use, or even waste the beauty of the world. And so we are locked inside the confines of our own concerns, with no access to the outside world. We have disestablished a continuity between ourselves and the outside, with no possibility for intimate communion and mutual enhancement. The world of the icon, though, restores this relationship by reminding us of what is outside and beyond, what ultimately gives value and vitality.

Before rendering material nature articulate by painting an icon, a traditional iconographer will fast and pray. Very often, the first image attempted, it is said, is that of the Transfiguration of Christ on Mt. Tabor. The iconographer aspires to achieve the inner vision of the world, an image of the world as intended by God. The *iconic* world, however, is not an unreal world; it is rather the real world which is called to ingress upon, and to spill over into this world. Orthodox iconography seeks to discover and then to disclose the reality of the experience of the heavenly kingdom in this world. In fact the icon articulates with theological conviction the faith in this kingdom and its activity in the earthly realm. Unfortunately we have desacralized, or denaturalized, this world by disconnecting it from *heaven*. The icon reverses perspective as we know it, and does away with the "objective" distance between this world and the next. There is no double order in creation. There is no sharp line of demarcation between *material* and *spiritual*. The icon constitutes the epiphany of God in the wood and the existence of the wood in the presence of God. It is neither idealism not idolatry. Like the unborn child in the womb of its mother, the icon presents to us the visible seeds of the divinity in the world. Its art and beauty represent God's Art and Beauty in the creation. The icon speaks in this world, yet in the language of the age to come. And therein lies the difference between religious art and iconography. Fr. Vasileios of Iviron further clarifies this distinction:

The one (a religious picture) is of this world. It speaks of this world and leaves you in this world. The other (a liturgical icon) brings you a simple, peaceful and life-giving message, coming down from above. ...It addresses itself to human nature universally, to human thirst for something beyond. Through the icon, an everlasting and unchanging reality speaks without words, a reality which, in the clarity of silence and in tranquillity, raises up from the deepest level, that which unites everything.[1]

The icon is an integral part of Orthodox spirituality, a central aspect of the celebration of creation. Like the Incarnation and the Creation, the icon is meant to be the piercing of space and time; that is, matter is met by God's eternal nature. The entire Church building–with its architecture, frescoes, and mosaics–does in space and matter what the liturgy does in time and praise: the anticipation of the heavenly kingdom and the participation of the divine presence. The seeming contradiction of an inaccessible God and a crucified Christ constitutes the ultimate measure of God's measureless love for the world. For, it is God's freedom that makes God's limitless love so powerful that it breaks all barriers and all limitations. The God who created out of love, who was incarnated out of love, now saturates the whole world with divine energies. And in Jesus Christ, God assumes a human face, the image of the suffering servant who has no beauty (cf. Isaiah 53:2) and yet whose beauty saves the world. Nothing renders the mystery of life more sensible than a human face, which announces an infinite transcendence and a profound presence.

The human face embraces both the level of freedom and the anguish of finitude, a grasping for the infinite and an enslavement to the finite. The icon reveals all the tensions, conflicts, and contradictions through which one is called to transparency; every fall is inscribed on it. But there is ultimately resurrection through communion, for to encounter Christ in the icon is to encounter an image beyond suffering, solitude, and hell, an image that will never die. Therefore, the basis of the icon is Christological, allowing the wholly inaccessible to be shared entirely. With the event of the Incarnation, as with the epiphany of the icon, the cycle of the non-representation of the Old Testament God (cf. Ex. 20:4-5, and John 1:18) is completed.

God became human that humanity might be deified, wrote the Christian Fathers.[2] The saints are those who emanate the light of deified humanity, while icons indicate the participation of humanity and the entire created world in divine life and light. As a result, faces of saints in icons are always frontal, *all eyes* (Macarius of Egypt), transparent, susceptive of divine energy. In the desert of fourth-century Egypt, Abba Bessarion said:

The monk ought to be as the Cherubim and the Seraphim: all eye.[3]

The profile in art signifies absence, and therefore sin. I see someone also means I am seen, and therefore I am in communion. In what is visible, I can experience the invisible. The icon constitutes a means of communion and through it I undergo an act of *pascha* (a passover, or passing over). It leads one through the charisma of the

Saint to the grace of the Spirit. It suggests one's own genuine image, the image that God created and that one is called to realize.

CREATOR AND CREATION

Since the doctrine of the divine Incarnation is at the heart of iconography, what is being represented is God's affirmation and assumption of the world. In color and on wood, the icon proclaims *God was made flesh* (John 1:14); to claim otherwise is to undermine the fullness the Incarnation and to deny Christ's humanity. The painting of icons, therefore, is not an incidental act of devotion or a pious option, but a necessary expression of the reality of both God and the world.

In his work entitled *On Divine Images*, John of Damascus, the eighth-century champion of icons, claims, *I do not adore creation in place of the creator, but I worship the One who became a creature.*[4] And since it is through matter that *God has worked out our salvation,*[5] there is an appropriate honor due to material things. I would argue that it is this sense of the salvific power of matter that we have lost today and which we need to rediscover. As John of Damascus writes:

Because of the Incarnation, I salute all remaining matter with reverence.

The icon exists within a particular framework of faith and worship. Often called *theology in color,* icons are inseparable from the liturgical and sacramental life of the

Church. The icon is the physical representation of the story of God's physical manifestation in both Christ and creation, and so *in honoring and venerating an icon, we receive sanctification.*[6] This holiness and transfiguration is communicated to the entire environment; for, sanctity has both a personal and a cosmic significance.

In the past, humanity has been understood as being superior to the rest of creation, singled out as belonging to a higher order, owing to man's reason and intellect. Indeed in the Western high middle ages, the *image of God* in the human person was identified with the rational nature. We have seen how an individualistic view of humanity has contributed greatly to the rise of our ecological problems. In the Greek Fathers' view, however, the *image of God* in humanity lay in its specific value of freedom. The human person must be associated with, and not dissociated from, the created world; for, it is through the human person that the created world must be transformed and offered to God. And so the world is freed from its natural limitations and becomes a bearer of life. In the words of Metropolitan John (Zizioulas) of Pergamon:

We believe that in doing this "in Christ" we, like Christ, act as priests of creation. When we receive these elements back, after having referred them to God, we believe that because of this reference to God we can take them back and consume them no longer as death but as life. Creation acquires for us in this way a sacredness which is not inherent in its nature but "acquired" in and through Man's free exercise of his imago Dei, i.e. his personhood. This distinguishes our attitude from all forms of paganism, and attaches to the human being an awesome responsibility for the survival of God's creation.[7]

This view of the priestly or para-priestly character of the human person was in earlier times acknowledged by Leontius of Cyprus (seventh century):

Through heaven and earth and sea, through wood and stone, through relics and Church buildings and the Cross, through angels and people, through all creation visible and invisible, I offer veneration and honor to the Creator and Master and Maker of all things, and to him alone. For the creation does not venerate the Maker directly and by itself, but it is through me that the heavens declare the glory of God, through me the moon worships God, through me the stars glorify him, through me the waters and showers of rain, the dew and all creation, venerate God and give him glory.[8]

Thus, an entire anthropology and cosmology are given artistic shape and utterance in the icon, the roots of which clearly lie in the spirituality and teachings of the Christian Church. This is why the two main events for Orthodox Iconography are the Incarnation and the Transfiguration. The first reforms what was *originally* deformed through sin and grants to the world the possibility of sanctification. The second realizes the consequences of divinization and grants to the world a foretaste even now of the beauty and light of the last times. We are, in this world, placed at a point of intersection between the present age and the future age, uniting the two at once. In his perceptive book, *The Sacred in Life and Art,* Philip Sherrard claims that the art of the icon presents holy personages:

...ready to convert the beholder from his restricted and limited point of view to the full view of their spiritual vision. For the art of the icon is ultimately so to transform the person who moves towards it that he no longer opposes the worlds of eternity and time, of spirit and matter, of the Divine and the human, but sees them united in one Reality, in that ageless image-bearing light in which all things live, move, and have their being. [9]

THE LIGHT THAT KNOWS NO EVENING

The light of an icon is an uncreated, sanctifying light, a light that is not of this world and knows no evening. Perspective is abolished, history is telescoped, and proportion is altered. The icon bears witness to a *different way of life.*[10] This life and light are shed from the Risen body of Christ and reveals the joy of the Resurrection.

Again Fr. Vasileios relates the beauty of icons to the luminous beauty of God, not by reason of nature's time and space, but because of the divine immanence of the created nature:

Icons depicting events which took place in daytime are no brighter that those showing us events which took place at night. The Last Supper and the prayer in Gethsemane are no darker than the Lord with the

Samaritan woman at Jacob's well, the Resurrection or Pentecost. The event depicted in an icon is not lit by the day or darkened by the night. Here all mortal flesh is silent. No element or event from the created world strikes a false note or operates in a worldly way or "takes the initiative," but everything serves its function in a restrained and priestly manner, undergoing the strange alteration of the Transfiguration. The icon neither needs the day nor fears the night. Night and day stand in need of the transfiguring power and grace of the icon. That is why they are represented by a symbol–the sun or the moon–in the world of iconography. And while the icon does not have need of anything, at the same time it does not despise anything. Here everything is blessed, and exults and leaps for joy. Everything is filled with uncreated light. That is why even events which took place in a house are always depicted in icons as being out of doors, spilling over the joy of salvation into all the world, shedding light upon all the nations...

The icon of the Transfiguration is no brighter than the icon of the Crucifixion. The Lord's face does not "shine" at the Transfiguration more than in any other icon of him. In iconography the Transfiguration is not an isolated and separate event, but a manifestation of the grace and mysterious illumination that fills everything and gives it life. All iconography is transfigured space, with a new order, structure and interpenetration. It is the world of the Transfiguration, the world of the uncreated illumination. So he who has spiritual sense can see the uncreated brilliance, invisible to the naked eye, that has glorified dark and bright alike. Light-colored faces are not invariably more pleasant and bright than those in deep and dark colors...

If the icon depicted night and day in romantic shades, it would leave us in the prison of the created world which we have come to know so well since the fall. If it feared the night, if it could be obscured by natural darkness, then we should be in the position of the unbaptized; we should fear death, and death would cut short our hope in life. We should remain in the territory of death...

The Lord's expression is calm and divinely peaceful as he sits on the foal of an ass, entering Jerusalem on the eve of the Passion. Later, when he is mocked and buffeted in the courtyard of the High Priest, he keeps the same undisturbed tranquillity, mingled with a deep sorrow at the consequences of sin for his creature. On the Cross, he preserves his serene glory from before the ages, which he had with God before the world was made (John 17:5).[11]

The art of iconography exacts objectivity, since it expresses the objective reality of the divine image; and it expects communion for it is not of some individual imagination or fantasy. The Orthodox tradition requires prayer and asceticism from the iconographer. For, pride and prejudice in the artist must be submitted to contemplation. The very material from which icons are made (wood, paint, and egg yolk–matter both mineral and organic) is not merely passive but has already been rendered dynamic by sanctification through the Incarnation.

Everything is filled with peace and light–clothing is illumined, animals, plants and rocks assume a paradisiac form. The luminous glory of God (Rev. 21:23) is everywhere–indeed the perspective of the kingdom is what gives meaning and truth to the present reality. Thus the perspective is often inverted, because one perceives with *the eye of the heart.*

The value of the icon is not paedagogical or aesthetic, but mystical or *sacramental.* It surpasses any opposition between this world and the next, uniting the two in an act of communion. It also transcends any opposition between figurative or non-figurative art, and appears instead as transfigurative. The icon presupposes and even proposes another means of communication, beyond the conceptual, written, or spoken word. It is the articulation or *writing out* (that is why the art is called *icono-graphy)* of what cannot be expressed in theology. The last book in the Bible is the Revelation. And revelation implies the manifestation of faces: it implies the certainty that humanity is called to *become God* and to become an icon.

"IN THE IMAGE AND LIKENESS OF GOD"

The human person, too, is an icon. Created in the image of God, humanity is also a living image of the created universe. The Church Fathers see humanity as existing on two levels simultaneously–on the level of spiritual and on the level of material creation. The human person is characterized by paradoxical dualities: humanity is limited yet free, animal yet personal, individual yet

social; in brief, created yet creative. To attempt escaping
this fundamental tension within humanity would be to
undermine the Christian doctrine of humanity created *in
the image and likeness of God* (Gen. 1:26) and as the
image of Jesus Christ who is at once human and divine.

A human being, says Gregory the Theologian (fourth
century), is like *another universe,*[12] standing at the center
of creation, mid-way between strength and frailty,
greatness and lowliness. Humanity is the meeting point
of all the created order. The idea of the human person as
a bridge, a point of contact and union, is developed as
early as the seventh century by the lay monk Maximus
Confessor.[13] As an image of the world, the human person
constitutes a microcosm. Another monastic writer, Nilus
of Ancyra (fifth century), makes this point very clearly:

*You are a world within a world... Look within yourself
and there you will see the entire world.*[14]

Gregory the Theologian, in the same homily quoted
above, also refers to the human person as an *icon of God,*
containing the *breath of God* (cf. Gen. 2:7). In fact, the
language used by the Christian classics to describe the
role of the human person often assumes a liturgical
character, and especially so when they speak of humanity
in its priestly function. The human person is able to
concentrate and consecrate everything to God.
Differences in created nature are no longer signs of
disunion but are effectively brought into union in their
inter-relatedness and in their reference to God.

Thus the world in its entirety forms part of the liturgy of heaven. Or, as we have already seen, the world constitutes a cosmic liturgy. God is praised by the trees and the birds, glorified by the stars and the moon (cf. Psalm 18:2), worshiped by the sea and the sand. There is a dimension of art, of music, and of beauty in the world. And the very existence of material creation constitutes a revelation of God (cf. Eph. 4:6), awaiting its liberation through the children of God (cf. Rom. 8:19). The world, then, becomes the clearest, albeit the most silent and inconspicuous sermon declaring the word of God, a sign of the kingdom of heaven, the bridal chamber (cf. Psalm 18) where God can touch the work of creation in the most intimate manner.

When Orthodox Christians enter a Church, they bow down before the altar, reverence the holy icons, bow to the minister, and lower their head at certain points of the liturgy. After receiving the Sacrament of the Eucharist, however, they depart bowing to none, for their conviction is that the life of the world and the heart of the Church are at that moment seeded and seated deeply within their own heart. When one is initiated into the mystery of the Resurrection and transformed by the light of the Transfiguration, then one understands the purpose for which God has created all things.[15] There is an Orthodox hymn in the Office of Matins (3rd Tone) that declares: *everything which receives the experience of the Resurrection is filled with joy.* Even the limitations of createdness betray not alienation from but attraction to God, and the world is rendered as a gift–a gift received from, and returned to, God. The climax of the Orthodox Liturgy is found in the words:

Your own from your own we offer to you, in all and through all.

Someone who sees the whole world as an icon experiences from this world the realities of the future and final resurrection. That person has already entered the life of resurrection and eternity. John Climacus, the abbot at St. Catherine's Monastery on Mt. Sinai, was convinced that, in the very beauty and beyond the shattered image of this world:

such a person always perceives everything in the light of the Creator God, and has therefore acquired immortality before the ultimate resurrection.[16]

There is a sense in which this person is indicating and anticipating here and now the transfiguration of the

world. The result is a prefiguration of the restored image of the world, a configuration in this world of uncreated and created elements.

THE WORLD AS ICON

There is an ancient text, the Life of St. Stephen the Younger (c. 764), that speaks of *the icon as a door.[17]* The significance of this is that the icon opens up to us and opens us up to a new reality. Divine light permeates and illumines all things, and articulates everything in divine praise. Ultimately, the whole architecture and symbolism of the Church becomes a *hymn of entry* into the heavenly kingdom: the musical chants, the liturgical gestures, the building bricks, the mosaic pieces, the candlelight, the incense fragrance. All share in the higher reality, all convey the content of the Christian faith in a variety of ways, appealing to each person in a unique but tangible manner.

By the same token, everything that is tangible in the world is a pointer forward and upward to the intangible. Preaching to a congregation in fourth-century Constantinople, Gregory the Theologian declared that:

Through what is accessible and known, God attracts us; while through what is inaccessible and unknown, God is marveled by us and desired still more ardently.[18]

Gradually the experience of awe and wonder is replaced with the certainty of the knowledge and with the recognition of God in all things created. This is the iconic understanding of the world where the *other* world penetrates and permeates *this* world, and where the eternal pierces the ephemeral. Thus the icon not only reflects true life and light, but even communicates and shares this life, thereby transforming reality and revealing the real aspect of the world. The earth as icon contains within itself the seeds of heaven.

THE ICON AS COMMUNION

When the Russian monk St. Andrei Rublev (c.1360-1430) painted his masterpiece *The Holy Trinity*–which depicts the Old Testament narrative of the three angels who visited Abraham and Sarah (cf. Gen. 18:1-33), and sometimes also known as *the hospitality of Abraham*–he was in fact representing the open communion of the triune Godhead, a love that is showered upon the face of the earth and in the hearts of people. In this respect, the icon is *not, as often supposed, a literal depiction of the Trinity*; the Old Testament prohibition against *graven idols* (Ex. 20: 4 and 34:17) always applies, at least with regard to God the Father and God the Holy Spirit. Instead, the Rublev icon must be understood as *an image of what the Trinity is*: a celebration and communication of life. This is why there is an empty or open place at the table of communion. The three persons of the Trinity are seated on three of the four sides of the rectangular table, allowing for or rather inviting the world to communion. Indeed, the very contours of their bodies create and reproduce in macro-image the communion chalice around which these angels are seated.[19] The potential sacredness of the world is more than a mere possibility; it is a vocation.

Everything in the world, to the slightest and most mundane detail of creation, is a sign of something. The second-century bishop of Lyons, Irenaeus, recognized that *nothing is a vacuum in the face of God. Everything is a sign of God.*[20] There is, in everyone and everything, a transparency that embraces both the transcendent and the immanent, revealing the transcendent reality in the most immanent. Inanimate objects become animated. The sun, the moon, and the waters assume human faces; death and hades are assigned human forms; everything acquires a personal dimension–just like people, just like God. The divine may therefore be encountered in and through the created world:

One God the Father of all, who is above all and through all and in all (Eph. 4:6).

The very earth that we tread becomes an icon, revealing God to us and indicating for us the way to God. Nothing whatsoever is neutral; nothing created lacks sacredness; no land is *terra incognita*. As we are reminded by Leonardo Boff:

The Fathers spoke of the mysteries and sacraments of the flesh of Christ.[21]

It is from this world and in this world that we are to receive *grace upon grace* (John 1:16) from the other world. In this created cosmos, just as in the world of the icon, we are to encounter Christ:

Everything is Christ's... He came to reveal the holiness in all things. All things are filled with him—yesterday, today, always.[22]

THE IMAGE OF CHRIST

There is no thing, no place, no time and no person that escapes, or is excluded from, the comprehensive love of Christ (cf. John 1:9). For Christ is God's categorical affirmation and assumption of the whole world. And there is, as a result, no condition, no tragedy, no experience outside the embrace of Christ. In all that we do and in all that we see, the aim is to respond to his command to follow him (cf. Matt. 19:24, Mark 10:21).

To be an imitator of Christ is to be assimilated to him. One can then walk on earth as Christ, and in the authority of Christ: *For it is not I who lives but Christ lives in me* (Gal. 2:20). Christ opens up an infinite perspective in himself and in us an infinite source of freedom.

All that one does is to be done with Christ: one suffers with him in order to be glorified with him (Rom. 8:17); one rises with him and sits with him in the kingdom (Eph. 2:6); one is alive with him (Eph. 2:5) and reigns with him (II Tim. 2:13); one lives with him and dies with him (II Tim. 2:11). In a word, one is totally *conformed to Christ* (Phil. 3:10). The words of St. Paul are anything but abstract; thus the phrases are meaningless unless there is a concrete sharing in the physical earthliness, in the flesh and blood of Christ. The phrase *in Christ* may be found over one hundred times in Pauline writings, and it implies not merely association with Christ but mystical and permanent union with Him, so that He becomes the air that we breath. *Let the remembrance of Jesus be united to your every breath*, writes John Climacus.[23] Thus with our every move and word, it is Christ that we seek and Christ that we manifest; when we pray, when we work, when we walk, when we write, when we speak, when we evangelize, when we are silent; it is Christ who is *the beginning, the way and the end* (Rev. 1:8). The Christian is not a professional, but a prophet; the Christian is not a slave, but a servant at the feet of Christ. A Christian is one who encounters Christ wherever he is sought, and this is what gives joy and life to the world.

The *Christ* dimension is also suggested in Orthodox icons of the enthroned Jesus, particularly in the truly magnificent mosaic of the late thirteenth century which survives in the Constantinopolitan Monastery of Chora (later known as *Kariye Cami*). The icon of Christ over the door to the nave is entitled: *The land ("chora") of the living.* The same notion of the resurrection of the dead or newness of life is envisaged in our personal spiritual life through the dynamic stage of for-give-ness *(syn-chore-sis)*, which implies foregoing oneself and *allowing room for others,* making space *(chora)* for the rest of the world, forgetting oneself and opening up in communion and acts of givenness. Nothing and none is excluded. Symeon the New Theologian poetically describes this co-habitation or co-indwelling of Christ in the world:

You make of all Your home and dwelling-place; You become a home to all, and we dwell in You.[24]

Everything therefore assumes a *Christ* dimension; everything is in some way sacramental. All depends on the receptiveness and openness of our heart. By the same token, everything is rendered unique, inasmuch as it has its particular place and meaning. Nothing is secular or profane; nothing is pagan or foreign. [25] Indeed, if God were not visibly present in the material creation, then we could not properly worship him as invisible. Were God not tangibly accessible in the very earthliness of this world, then he would not be the loving, albeit transcendent author of the universe. This is surely the implication of the basis of the Christian faith, namely that *the Word assumed [or became] flesh* (John 1:16), which we all too often, in a reductionist manner, take to mean *became human.* Yet the early Christian writers categorically stated that, *what God did not assume, God did not heal.*[26] What God did not reach out and touch, did not come down and sanctify, cannot possibly be related to or loved by God. And unless Christ may be discovered *in the least of his brethren* (Matt. 25:40) and in the least particle of matter, then he is too distant to matter. There is a wonderful saying attributed to Jesus, which expresses the reality of his presence everywhere:

Lift up the stone, and there you will find me, cleave the wood, and I am there.[27]

Matter is not merely an object for our possession and exploitation. The earth has not only economic but also moral and sacramental value. For *the earth and all its fullness* (Psalm 23:1) is a bearer of God, a place of encounter with Christ, the very center-point of our salvation. To close with the words of Leonardo Boff:

All things are sacraments when viewed in God's perspective and light. The word, human beings, and things are signs and symbols of the transcendent.[28]

THEOLOGY IN COLOR

Thus the theological statement made by the icon is threefold:

(i) that the world was created good, and therefore must be loved; (ii) that at the Incarnation, Christ assumed a

human body, thereby affirming the intrinsic value of the whole created world; and (iii) that salvation embraces all of created matter, as well as the human body and soul.

This is the world and teaching of the icon: that the entire world is an icon. The whole of creation constitutes an icon painted before all ages, an image eternally engraved by the unique iconographer of the Word of God, namely the Holy Spirit. This image is never totally destroyed, never fully effaced. Our aim is simply to reveal this image in the heart and to reflect it in the world. Yet the image itself, the icon, is indelible. For the world has been forever *sealed with the gift of the Holy Spirit.*[29] In our age, green is perhaps most fittingly the color of the Holy Spirit, recalling as it does Greek patristic thought,[30] while indicating the renewal of life itself and the revival of all things.

CHAPTER EIGHT

Sophia–the Wisdom of God

I, wisdom, was the daily delight of the Lord...rejoicing in the inhabited world and delighting in the human race (Prov. 8:30-31)

INTRODUCTION

A particular question arises in our time when we consider the issues of God's relationship with creation and the sacredness of the world. I refer here to the concept of the wisdom of God, particularly as it–or rather as she (because *hokh' ma* in Hebrew and *sophia* in Greek are feminine terms)–is personified in the wisdom literature of the Bible. Indeed, even the characteristics of *sophia* have been clearly personified as feminine from as early as biblical times, and it has today become popular to view *sophia* as the divine feminine *par excellence*. This has been the understanding not only of a number of contemporary theologians, especially feminist writers, but also of certain Orthodox thinkers, most notably the Russian theologian Fr. Sergius Bulgakov (1871-1944).

Bulgakov was Professor of Political Economy at Moscow University and, later, Dean of St. Sergius's Theological Institute in Paris. One of the most charismatic and creative Orthodox theologians in the twentieth century, Bulgakov belonged to a group of intellectuals who converted from Marxism to Christianity on the eve of the 1917 Russian Revolution. As early as 1912, he published his Philosophy of Economics, where he first attempted a systematic formulation of his sophiology. He was concerned to develop a world-view that was both consistent with the Orthodox tradition and able also to meet the challenge of contemporary technology.

Although the formulations of Bulgakov regarding the significance and place of *sophia* in Christian theology and cosmology leave much to be desired–particularly with regard to his elaboration of its relationship to the traditional doctrines of the Holy Trinity and the Incarnation–the contribution of this great thinker surely lies in his grappling with the critical issues of our time, specifically with the concept of God's communion with the created world. We shall, therefore, examine the notion of *sophia* irrespective and independently of the metaphysical system developed by Bulgakov or by any other particular writer. At all events, there is in the Orthodox tradition no unique or uniform formulation of the sophiological theory.

Now the first point that needs to be made is that the concept of *sophia* is not an obscure esoteric doctrine related to gnosticism or theosophy. Neither is it an idea characteristic solely of Russian religious consciousness, as some may believe.[1] What is connected to Russian philosophical thought exclusively is the identification–and that only after the sixteenth century–of *sophia* with Mary, the Mother of God. This is the opinion of Vladimir Solovyev (1853-1900), Pavel Florensky (1892-1943) and Bulgakov himself. But this is not the complete picture, for in the Greek tradition *sophia* is identified rather with Christ. It is understood as the unity of heaven and earth, a unity that is most profoundly and uniquely held together in the divine-human person of Jesus Christ, as the eternal Word and Creator who always lovingly assumed creation. It is the unity that holds all things in one.

In the West, *sophia* is normally identified with the Mother of God, at least as an accommodating symbol, while the primary typological interpretation remains the identification of *sophia* with Christ. This in a way *solves* the problem; but the imaginative reflection on the agent and action of Sophia nonetheless continues to arouse fascination.

SOPHIA AND THE VIRGIN MOTHER OF GOD

The double emphasis or ambivalence in Orthodox spirituality–where the Russian tradition relates *sophia* to the Virgin Mother, the Greek tradition relates sophia to the Incarnate Word–is by no means fortuitous. It cannot be an accident of interpretation that certain early Russian Churches are dedicated to the divine *sophia* in honor of the all-holy Virgin Mary, whereas the finest example of Greek Byzantine architecture, the Church of Hagia Sophia in Constantinople, is dedicated to Jesus Christ as the divine Word. Together, Christ and Mary reveal two equally significant aspects of the divine wisdom; together they bear the secret and reflect the sacrament of God's relationship with the world. The Church (as the body of Christ) and Mary (as the living temple of God) are intimately and even innately connected with that divine feminine known as *sophia*. And as such, they disclose aspects of divine love in creation and redemption. In this respect, *sophia* should not be conceived as a *woman* in contradistinction to the *word* who is a *man*. Rather, it means that divine *sophia* contains the qualities of creating, redeeming, and sustaining. And in this way, *sophia* contains the qualities of wisdom seen in either feminine or masculine terms: it is the one who can judge without hatred or bias, as well as love without condition. The two sides belong together: just as man and woman, earth and heaven, Logos and Sophia. We are once again in the duality that demands communion. Perhaps, then, the two icons on either side of the Royal Doors at the sanctuary in an Orthodox Church show the the inner and the outer *faces* of the Word of God–the *divine Logos* and the *Sophia aeterna*.

This cosmological role of the Virgin Mary, as the parallel and even the premise of the cosmic event of Christ, has been creatively advanced in recent times by the late Philip Sherrard:

*This is the secret of the term Mother of God (Theotokos), as it is also the secret of the initial cosmogonic act. The Mother of God is the Virgin Mother or the unconditioned holy Wisdom–*Sophia aeterna–*through whom God reveals* *himself to himself by manifesting the virtualities of his divine Names, the prototypes of all created being latent in his unknown and transcendent Being. It is the revelation by means of which God acquires his Godhood.* [2]

The Virgin Mother therefore embraces created and uncreated in a manner corresponding to that in which Jesus Christ assumes divinity and humanity *without confusion and yet without division.*[3] She becomes the "Mater" from which all matter is born–Sherrard refers to her as *universal nature, natura naturans*–and the matrix in whom all matter flowers:

Although she is one, she exists in two modes, eternal and temporal, uncreated and created... She is Earth as a single immaterial feminine divinity, and she is earth as a manifold, material reality. She is herself the Body of the cosmic Christ, the created matrix in whom the divine Logos eternally takes flesh. She is the bridge that unites God to the world, the world to God, and it is she that bestows on the world its eternal and sacred value. She is the seal of its sacred identity.[4]

Now in order to appreciate how Mariology reveals the femininity of creation, one must turn to the powerful symbolism of iconography and to the profound semantics of liturgy. In Orthodox Churches from the late fourth century, the Virgin Mary is depicted in the apse immediately above the altar, somewhere between heaven and earth. She constitutes the bridge and the link between the One who creates and *contains all things* (Christ the

Pantokrator) and the world. In comparison to the inaccessible, transcendent God, the Virgin Mary is arguably the person more immediately accessible and more frequently resorted to in daily prayer and devotion. Thus, in the popular Orthodox Service of the *Akathist Hymn* (early seventh century), the *Theotokos* is hailed as:

the throne of the King, as bearing the One who bears the universe...as the womb of the divine Incarnation, and as the one through whom creation is refashioned...as the heavenly ladder by which God descended, the bridge that leads the earthly to the heavenly...(Stasis I). In her, the heavens rejoice with earth and the earth concelebrates with heaven... She is the shelter of the world, broader than the clouds (Stasis II), the promised land, the land of the infinite God, the key of Christ's kingdom and the hope of eternal blessings (Stasis III).

She is not, however, separated from the earthly and created; she is described as *the rock that refreshes those who thirst for life, the tree of life, the robe, the river, the tower.*

Through Mary, therefore, we learn something about what God is and why creation exists. We discover how *God is love* (I John 4:18), and how it is that the world hears and bears the seed of the divine Word. As the living temple of God, the Virgin Mother reminds us that we too are *the temple of God* (I Cor. 3:16 and II Cor. 6:16), that our *body is also the temple of the Holy Spirit within* (I Cor. 6:19), and that the whole world is a temple inasmuch as it is a sign of the presence of God. In fact, it has been revealed to us that *the Pantokrator God is the temple itself* (Rev. 21:22).

It is not by accident that, in Orthodox Church decoration, the icon of Mary the *Platytera* (the one who is *more spacious* than the whole of creation) is placed beneath the icon of the *Pantokrator* (the one who *holds all* of creation). Beside the *sophia* of the divine Word stands *the vessel of divine wisdom,* that treasury and repository of divine *sophia.* The unceasing response to God's eternal initiative is the continual *yes* of the Virgin. Mary's word constantly and completely corresponds to God's Word, lovingly bearing that Word in her womb and selflessly confirming it in her life. She is the encompassing of any duality.

Mary is able to realize these *mysteries* precisely because, again in the words of the Akathist hymn, *she has yoked together maidenhood and motherhood...remaining a virgin, yet giving birth* (Stasis III). As virgin, she heals the brokenness of the world; as mother, she fulfills the barrenness of creation. As virgin, she signifies the integrity of life, and not just of celibacy; as mother, she personifies the affirmation of life, and not just of marriage. The same hymn states that *she brings opposites to unity.* Little wonder that the Virgin Mother is held in high esteem by monastic and married persons alike. She rightly constitutes the queen *(ánassa)* of heaven, as well as the breath *(anássa)* of creation.

SOPHIA AND THE WORLD

The world as a revelation of divine wisdom and glory is the fundamental theme of the Christian philosophy and worldview. Everything bears the seed of God, and it is the immanence of God in creation that lies at the center of wisdom theology. The very ground of this world is the wisdom of God and cannot be comprehended–or even apprehended–apart from God. Thus *sophia* is the intelligible basis of creation. It is through *sophia,* especially as it is manifested in Jesus and Mary, that we are able to comprehend creation at all.

According to this Christian philo-sophy (*love of wisdom)* or sophio-logy (*study of wisdom*), everything temporal finds its true meaning and derives its ultimate value in the light of the eternal. The eternal image of divine *sophia* is that which leaves in the temporal world the imprint and image of God. According to an Orthodox hymn sung at the feast of the Dormition of the Virgin Mother of God (August 15): *The wisdom of God is the creative and unitive power in all things.*

Discerning in creation the wisdom of God is discovering the royal path between two extreme poles in our attitude to the world. For on the one hand there is a latent world-denying outlook which is known as *manicheism,* while on the other hand there is a prevailing world-worshipping outlook which is known as *pantheism.* The first makes too sharp a separation between the two; the result is an undermining of the world. The second blurs the line of demarcation between God and the world, thereby almost equating the two; the result is an overemphasis of the world. These attitudes are also common to Christians who lean either toward an anti-cosmic attitude that despises the world or toward a servility to the world. Both are detrimental to the image of the world and of ourselves.

What is crucial at this point is a reinterpretation of the doctrine of the Incarnation, the roots of which arise from the innermost depths of the Holy Trinity and penetrate into the very heart of heaven and earth. Such a Trinitarian basis involves the descent and abiding presence of the Holy Spirit in the world. Thus *sophia* is the contemplative inspiration and interpretation (*theoria*) of the world and of its destiny:[5] it is a *dialectical* balance between opposing extremes, an *ascetic* relationship with the world and with God.

For Bulgakov:

this can be accomplished only through a change in our conception of the world and through a sophianic perception of the world in the Wisdom of God. This alone can give us strength for new inspiration, for new creativity, for overcoming the mechanization of life.[6]

This *change,* however, is not accomplished easily. It is a radical conversion or reversal of attitude likened in the monastic tradition to *a constant violent action against the trend of our nature.*[7] Paradoxically, if this violence against our own nature does not occur, then what inevitably does occur is the rape of nature around us. Somewhere or other the *cost* must be borne. Somewhere or other responsibility must be assumed–in the world and for the world.

SOPHIA AND THE WORD

Divine Wisdom is the revelation of the divine Word. For the Logos is the all-embracing unity *through whom all things were made* (cf. John 1:3) and *in whom all things are* (cf. Rom. 11:36). And it is this which constitutes the Christian worldview: the world is in God, despite the fact that it exists outside of God. The world belongs to God, in spite of its being wholly *other* than God. This is neither dualism nor pantheism, but Christian panentheism: it recognizes that *the identity and distinction, the unity and duality of sophia in God and in creation, rest on the same foundation.*[8] In this way, therefore, *sophia* is connected to the Logos, the great Word of God. Everything in the world signifies the same truth, says the same thing, points to the same end: from the *I am* of God's Word addressed to Moses in the burning bush, to the great *I am* sayings of the Incarnate Word of Jesus recorded in the Gospels.

There is an interconnectedness in all things that is in turn most profoundly connected to the divine Word (Col. 1:17 and Eph. 1:10), a positive *fiat* or *yes* to all that is God's. According to an Orthodox hymn sung three times at the Great Blessing of the Waters during the Feast of Theophany (January 6):

The voice of the Lord on the waters cries aloud saying: Come all of you, and receive the Spirit of wisdom, the Spirit of understanding...from Christ who is made manifest.

The Judaeo-Christian concept of *sophia,* particularly as it is developed in the Wisdom literature of the Hebrew Scriptures (certainly in Proverbs, Wisdom, and Ecclesiasticus), has perhaps been influenced to some extent by Greek, Egyptian, and Persian thought. And the theological pinnacle of Hellenistic Jewish writings is attained by the author of the Wisdom of Solomon, whose most original contribution lies in his virtual identification of *sophia* and *spirit:*

I called on God, and the spirit of wisdom came to me (7:8).⁹ This sophia is unique, manifold, and subtle (7:23), pervading and penetrating all things (7:24), ordering all things well (8:1).

The spirit of wisdom is more than simply the immanence or all-pervading presence of God that fills the world. It is a gift from above, reflecting in its very immanence the transcendence of God:

While remaining in herself, she renews all things (7:27).

The author of this pseudonymous work is very explicit on this point:

She is a breath of the power of God, and a pure emanation of the glory of the Almighty...an image of divine goodness (7:25-26).

Revealing *sophia* as the *image (*or *icon) of God's goodness* this kind of personification further associates

Wisdom with the creative Word of God. Thus we read in Solomon's prayer for wisdom:

O God...who have made all things by your word, and by your wisdom have formed humankind (9:1).

In the same way, New Testament writings will depict Jesus as Wisdom; for he is the final incarnation of the eternal Word and Spirit of Wisdom, the embodiment of divine truth and revelation. As a result of this understanding, Orthodox iconographic representations of Wisdom texts sometimes depict the Wisdom-Angel, that is Christ as Angel (especially in earlier centuries) while at other times portray the Wisdom-Christ. As symbolic representations, they expressed a more naturalistic and almost humanistic approach which were unacceptable by some in the sixteenth century, such as the monk Euthymius who declared outrightly:

The hypostatic Wisdom, as the Word and Power, is the Son of God. And if one dares to paint wisdom under an invented form, one will soon begin to dare painting the Word by means of another invention... [And] what could be more absurd than that?[10]

It is precisely the Christological definition of the Council of Chalcedon (in 451 CE) that provides the key to and the Christian justification of sophiology. This definition speaks of divine and human natures as being united in the one person of Christ *unconfusedly, unchangeably, inseparably, and undividedly.* Notice how the Chalcedonian formula merely comprises four negative propositions telling us how not to think of the relationship between Christ's divine and human natures. *The positive meaning of the formula, the Chalcedonian yea is...the bequest of the Patristic age to future generations, and it is our duty to work at it.*[11] Both historically and theologically, the Chalcedonian definition offered no final solution to the way in which God relates to the world. It required, and still requires, interpretation on our part.

CONCEALED MYSTERY AND COSMIC MYSTERY

The starting point of any sophiological philosophy is the basic appreciation of the world as reflecting and conforming to the image of God. Thus the criterion must be positive theology, not negative thinking. *Positive or kataphatic theology* constitutes, at least partly, the endeavor to reach God through creation and concerns the revelation of God through creation. It regards God not as wholly incommunicable and transcendent, but as communicating through creation and drawing all creatures towards the divine. *Negative thinking or the apophatic way* implies negation rather than affirmation. It is the recognition that God lies above and beyond every image. Kataphatic images must be denied or *stripped down* in order for creation to penetrate behind and beyond the symbol to Reality. According to the positive theological method, those images sanctioned by Scripture are superior. However, with apophatic methodology, even those symbols which have no apparent similarity with the divine Reality may claim superiority.

Sophiology, for example, adheres to the kataphatic method: *God has drawn his image in the creature; consequently, this image of God can be represented.*[12] For Bulgakov, this *image of God in the world is heavenly humanity,* namely Sophia. And this Sophia is eternally divine-human;[13] hence the centrality of the doctrine of the Incarnation. Bulgakov notes elsewhere:

God has created the world precisely for his Incarnation; it is not the world which, through the fall of man, has impelled God to become incarnate.[14]

This broader and certainly more appealing approach to the Incarnation is characteristic generally of Orthodox thought and specifically of the Eastern Church Fathers. The Incarnation is conceived as the expression of the eternal love of God, who wishes to be associated with creation in the most intimate manner possible.

The weakness of the sophiological world-view may lie in the way it modifies apophatic theology and consequently undermines the transcendence of God. For there remains, in the very expression and event of Incarnation, an *untold* reality and an *unknown* quality. To be *negative* is actually to make space and to allow for God, to defer to the unboundedness of God. This is the knowing that is also an unknowing; it is knowing that one does not know.

It has been observed that sophiology primarily adheres to the kataphatic method, but the apophatic standpoint is not altogether absent from the wisdom texts:

Where then does wisdom come from? And where is the place of understanding? It is hidden from the eyes of all living, and concealed from the birds of the air... But God understands the way to it, and knows its place (Job 28:20, 21, 23).

Negative language is essential in appreciating the *way* and the *place* of wisdom; for despite the volumes written about the ineffable and the transcendent, it often remains inapplicable to its object. The prologue to the Gospel of John has been frequently misunderstood and given way to almost any form of theology, especially that of there being nothing incomprehensible within the scope of theology as a result of the Incarnation. In this case, apophatic theology provides a crucial corrective. For to be *negative* is to undertake enquiry without the presumption of full knowledge. Orthodox Christian theology understands the paradox at the very center of this methodology. It is this paradox which accounts for the *distinction* between divine essence and energies, although one must first learn how to recover this theology from its current reputation of irrelevance and obfuscation.

Orthodox theology has always exhibited a bi-polar attitude towards creation, striving to preserve the tension between divine transcendence and divine immanence in relation to the world. The doctrine of the distinction between God's essence and energies calls for respect towards the divine mystery in its complexity. Accordingly, the unknown God remains hidden and unchanged in divine fullness, but is manifested in an infinite variety of loving acts. The energies are neither God's essence nor divine nature, because God is not bound but rather chooses to reach out. And God does so in ecstasy (which literally means standing outside of oneself: *ek-stasis)* to a nature of another order. The Greek word for "energy" (*en-ergeia*) signifies work (*ergon*), action, operation, or power (*dynamis*). Thus energies are distinguished from essence not because they are modified or less concentrated, but primarily because they presuppose the existence of a free and personal God. They manifest the goodwill of God, divine grace, or mercy.

A theology that cannot express and explain the paradoxical distinction between the essence and energies of God, may also prove incapable of accepting any real relationship between temporal creature and the eternal Creator. Such a theology moves no further than philosophical existentialism or social humanitarianism. Yet the more God is *humanized,* that is to say, the more one struggles to understand the mystery of the Incarnation, and the more one places creation on its proper level, the more majestic and mysterious the understanding of creation becomes. The most tangible illustration of God's love is the divine descent into a relationship with creation and the rendering of divine absoluteness inaccessibly absolute. *God is* means *God is love* (I John 4:18), which also implies that the "world is loved." The entire world is a *burning bush* of God's energies, pregnant with divine life. Time is a ladder set up by God in order that creation may ascend towards heaven, and upon which God descends through divine energies to the temporal human being and the ephemeral world. God, however, is neither divine essence nor divine energy–God does not need to become in order to manifest divine fullness. Time, space, the body, and the world are creations springing from God's desire for human persons to become gods by grace.

The Incarnation must be viewed in this perspective not only as a phase, but as a culmination of a series of phases in this double movement of descent and ascent. In one and the same person, human temporality and divine eternity are united and conformed in a way never before realized. In Christ, since there is no interval between the offering of divine love and the response of human love, divine *kenosis* provokes within humanity certain effects which are termed virtues: humility, kindness, purity of thought, love. *The essence of all* [*virtue*] *is our Lord Jesus Christ* (cf. I Cor. 1:30). In con-descending to descend and to assume human form, God reveals the value of humanity called to deification. The human person, whose image Christ assumes, takes on the image of Christ and lives in Christ ... or, Christ in them (cf. Gal. 2:20). Such a person reflects Christ, strives to become the image of Christ, and even becomes Christ. Such a person holds together, albeit by grace, the very same poles united by Christ, namely the *two natures in one person, unconfusedly, unchangeably, inseparably, and undividedly.* Thus Symeon the New Theologian wrote of his spiritual elder, Symeon the Pious:

*He possessed the whole of Christ, and was himself
completely Christ... Everything for him was Christ, as
if clothed entirely with Christ.*[15]

In its fundamental distinction between divine essence
and divine energies, Orthodox theology sees the very
presupposition of all knowledge of God, as well as of the
world, without which it would be very easy to resort to
the rational connection between cause and effect as the
only possible relationship between God and the world.
The acceptance of this distinction denotes an
understanding of God and divine truth in terms of
personal relationship and of knowledge in terms of
personal participation. This element of personal
communion and communication raises further the issue
of the importance of one's relationship with other people,
and particularly with the one who actually imparts this
spiritual wisdom.

THE WISDOM OF THE SPIRITUAL ELDER

The spiritual elder as the image of Christ is the one who
enables us to view the world in a balanced way, avoiding
the naive optimism which underlines the original
perfection of creation (which we may label the Pelagian
view), as well as the destructive pessimism which
emphasizes the original corruption of creation (which we
may label the Augustinian view). The relationship with
one's spiritual elder serves as a bridge between Creator
and creation, relating as it does the transcendent God
with the immanent world. For the human person is called

to know and to become God, and this dynamic reality is made possible through the spiritual guide who is deified and who deifies.[16]

This experience of the oneness between God and the world–inasmuch as it overcomes the fundamental errors of pantheism and dualism–implies a personal understanding and undergoing. That is, one needs to know for oneself. One must discover for oneself the insight that comes from loving God and the world *with all one's heart* and *as oneself* (cf. Mark 12:30-1). For we meet *sophia* in whoever can perceive creation as *the house of wisdom* (Prov. 9:1). This is like *the knowing of knowing* (a phrase which, from Aristotle to Hegel, has served as a philosophical definition of God). But one cannot come to know by oneself. Just as a child learns to speak from someone else, so too the language of heaven is taught by someone else. The spiritual elder is precisely one such initiator, who imparts the knowledge of truth and instructs one in the skill of seeing the same world with different eyes. The aim is to empower people *to see God and to contemplate God even in this world*.[17]

From his own experience of the Staretz Ambrose, Dostoevsky offers a more contemporary description of the wise elder:

What is such an elder? An elder is one who takes your soul, your will, into his soul and his will. When you choose an elder, you renounce your own will and yield it to him in complete submission, complete self-negation.

This novitiate, this terrible school of abnegation, is undertaken voluntarily, in the hope of self-negation, of self-mastery, in order after a life of obedience, to attain to perfect freedom, that is from self; to escape the lot of those who have lived their whole life without finding their true selves in themselves.[18]

Such elders merited the title pneumatophoros or *Spirit-bearer* because they strove to be led and to lead as perfectly as possible through the immediate guidance of the Holy Spirit, rather than through individual powers or ambitions. The genuine spiritual elder is a leader because he or she assists in the rebirth and regeneration of the Christian into the life of the Spirit.

By relating to such a person as a spiritual elder, one reaches the *great understanding* of a radical conversion (*metanoia*).[19] For, if we cannot relate properly to what we can see, how can we relate to that which is unseen (cf. I John 4:20)? The relationship with the spiritual elder is a paradigm of the relationship desired with God, a preparation and attuning of one's capacity to become open to the grace of God in the world. Ultimately, it is not so much the elder who speaks, but the Spirit of God who works within (cf. Matt. 10:20). Knowing therefore implies being known (cf. Gal. 4:9); understanding means being understood by another person; and loving primarily signifies being loved. *For God so loved the world...* (John 3:16)

In this respect, the spiritual elder is a charismatic inspirer who transmits wisdom, Christ Himself, in a relationship with disciples. Such a person seeks to give nothing of self, but rather of Christ who lives within (cf. Gal. 2:20). *To everyone I give only what God tells me to give,* said St. Seraphim of Sarov, a beloved staretz of the Orthodox Church.[20]

Obedience to a spiritual leader is emphasized from the very origins of Orthodox monasticism. It has always been understood that the figure of the spiritual elder illustrates the two levels on which the Church exists and functions: the hierarchical and the spiritual, the outward and the inner, the institutional and the inspirational. In this sense, the elder (*geron* in Greek, *staretz* in Russian) exists alongside the apostles. Although not necessarily ordained through the episcopal laying on of hands, the spiritual elder is essentially a prophetic person who has received the charisma of discernment directly from the Spirit of God. The difference, then, between the apostle, the spiritual elder, and ourselves lies in the degree of wisdom, not in the quality or potential of being.

"SOPHIA: LET US BE ATTENTIVE"

The vision of *sophia* and of her beauty is the vision of a transfigured world beyond the damage or distortion of the temporal world. It is an eternal beauty that transcends the sphere of this world and yet is also discerned within this world. By *sophia* is meant the archetypal image of creation (which is the ideal world created in and by the

Logos) and the active heart of this world (which is the same body of Christ, the incarnate Logos). The world thus appears as an extension in matter and time of the embodiment of the eternal Logos, just as the Church is a prolongation of the body of Jesus Christ. It is hardly surprising that, only after generations of theologians and local councils had deliberated, did the early Church decide on the relationship of the eternal Logos to the incarnate Christ. In the final analysis, even the doctrine itself was a conscious ambiguity, a deliberate questioning of the relationship of the uncreated Word to the created world.

Such is the cosmological function of *sophia:* it is a bridge between God and the world, belonging to and uniting both realities at once. As the creative and unitive Word of God, it is also the divine Wisdom whose seeds and traces may be found in the multiplicity of creation. It is the uncreated beauty of God revealed and reflected in the beauty of creation. *One in God, she is many in creation,* was the way Florensky described *sophia.*[21]

This offers us a valid alternative to the dichotomies with which we are often confronted, between either God or the world. The theory of *sophia* enables us to avoid the sharp line of demarcation or dichotomy between heaven and earth. For *sophia* is not simply the transcendence of God in contrast to the world; it is the immanence of God in relation to the world. This equally safeguards the "otherness" of God and overcomes the dangers of pantheism in the *affinity* of God; for between Creator and creation, there is both distinction and identity. *Sophia* is both the divinity of God and the createdness of creation, yet more: for it is also the *createdness* of God and the divine spark within creation. *Sophia* preserves the luminosity and numinosity of God and creation alike. And sophiology represents much more than an aesthetical or mystical experience of the world's beauty; it reveals the world as a place of encounter with the personal God.

Sin and abuse have obscured but not obliterated this reality. Through the grace of the divine-human Word and Wisdom of God, there is potential for recognizing the beauty of "sophia" within and beyond the shattered image of our world. This Word/Wisdom is incarnate in the person of Jesus Christ and, by extension, is present in the Church as the body and bride of Christ. The Hebrew Scriptures long ago recognized that:

Truly...that is wisdom, to depart from evil. That is understanding (Job 28:28).

This in turn means that the personified "sophia" remains personal. But the wisdom of a guiding elder is crucial in educating and maturing persons able to discern the beauty of God in the world. For, in the words of Solovyev:

The entire worldly and historical process is the process of the realization and incarnation [of the eternal feminine principle] in a great diversity of forms and degrees.[22]

The Orthodox doctrine concerning the essence and energies of God is of vital importance in avoiding the accusations leveled against Bulgakov and the other Russian sophiologists, who were said to render *sophia* either an uncreated fourth person of the Trinity or else one created aspect of the world (pantheism). For this doctrine is sympathetic to the principle of divine presence in the world, while rejecting both the divinity of the world and the inaccessibility of God to the world.

God is therefore present in everything and is recognized in the divine energies everywhere. Such an understanding safeguards both the freedom and gratuitousness of divine love, and the dependence on God of a creation, which has freedom and choice. The gift of the divine energies presupposes permanent cooperation, mutual correspondence, and intimate communion. Participation in the divine energies closes the distance and division between God and world, while at the same time disclosing the distinction between the two. The dialectic of created and uncreated is finally resolved on the level of desire–the will to love God as the source of life. The divine *sophia* is perceived only in the dialectic of discontinuity and continuity, of rupture and relation, of dissociation and association–namely in the affirmation of the unknowable essence of God and in the aspiration to the knowable energies of God that penetrate and permeate the whole world.

Thus before every person and animal, before each bird and insect, before all trees and mountains and waters, the words of the Orthodox liturgy are pertinent: *Sophia: Let us arise and be attentive!*

CHAPTER NINE

The Privilege of Despair

*Our privilege is the unrelenting effort of renewal of sight and hope
out of failure...*
*Our privilege is our sorrow: to know by blindness, by falling short,
the magnanimity of the world...*
*And grief alone is measure of the love
that only lives by rising out of graves...1*

This chapter might well have been entitled *The Problem of Evil,* since the following pages will endeavor to look from a spiritual perspective at the desperate global situation that we are facing. In the current environmental crisis, it is no wonder that we fail to recognize the beauty in the decay, the life in the dying that surrounds us.

The frightening thing is that, despite pretensions to liberalism, one of the reasons for this failure is that our world is quite intolerant toward weakness, sin, and death. We have, it seems, lost the perception of renewal and repentance and have, therefore, become insensitive to the power of forgiveness. As a result, we have deprived ourselves of the vision of wholeness and holiness. Earlier periods recognized and held together more closely the paradox of beauty and ugliness in the world, of humanity *created in the divine image* and yet also *fallen,* of progress and regress, of development and destruction, of life and death. It is crucial to look upward to our source and destiny, while also looking downward to our reality and predicament. *We must neither lower our sights nor sever our roots.*[2] Both our divine distinction and our destructive defects are part and parcel of our human dignity. In the words of that Syrian ascetic, Isaac of Nineveh, who experienced in the abyss of his heart the grandeur and ignominy of creation:

There is nothing more powerful than despair. For despair cannot be conquered by anything...because then God gives us salvation, strength, and rest.[3]

Our disgrace, however, must be confronted and comforted. Just as speaking of the presence of God in all things (and of heaven and earth as being full of God's glory [cf. Jer. 23:24]) does not imply that God is all things,[4] similarly it does not mean that all things are as God wills. We cannot pretend that nothing has happened or hope that we can turn back time. God's grace comes not by taking away our weakness but by taking the latter more seriously. This implies an unfolding of a new relationship with our world. Accordingly, the same Isaac says:

The grace which raised us up after we had sinned is greater than that given when we were not in existence, which brought us into creation.[5]

STEP ONE–THE ACT OF CONFESSION

Repentance is the natural rhythm of life. The first step in repentance is confrontation or confession, not denial and repression. The most mystical of all experiences is the profound realization of who we are, of what we have done, and of where we are headed. Our destruction stays with us as a reminder of our destructiveness. The repercussions of our sin occur on global, local, and personal levels. We are *privileged* to know all too well the effects, for instance, of the world debt crisis on international poverty. Although Christian leaders have not always bothered to interpret them *theologically,* acts of aggression are well-documented–the raping of nature, of women, and of children. Herein lies the dynamic interpretation of *original sin,* as the Christian Church propounds it: as a result of the *fall,* our aggression and propensity towards sin is a part of us. From now on, both good and evil, love and hatred, compassion and suffering *grow together until the harvest* (Matt. 13:30). There will of course be, as we believe, a radical and ultimately transforming harvest, but until that time and until that apocalypse, we must disabuse ourselves of the romantic notion that Christianity is about *another* or a *better* world. Christianity is about this world–"wheats and weeds" (Matt. 13:25f.), warts and all–this entire world entirely transfigured in God. Even the idealist Augustine of Hippo (d. 430) was able to entertain this inclusive concept:

I no longer desired a better world, because I was thinking of creation as a whole.[6]

It is time we began considering salvation less as a damnation of a certain part (smaller or larger) and more as the integration and reconciliation of all things in Christ. We have been forbidden to judge and commissioned to heal. Salvation then must be considered on broader, more universal terms–not restricted to the individual, but embracing a community, and thus social or ecclesial. Likewise, it is not restricted to humanity but extends to the whole of creation: it is, therefore, cosmic. *No one is saved alone, but in unity with all* people and all things.[7] I think it is characteristic of the Orthodox attitude towards salvation that it is likewise fearlessly open-ended, including soul and body, humanity and creation, animate and inanimate.

It bears reiteration that first of all we must recognize we are the ones who have in fact shattered the image, not created it. We are not the *good Samaritans,* but the *highway robbers* (cf. Luke 10:29f.). It is wrong for us to presume that we have cared for this world; that would be unacceptable self-righteousness. The beauty of the image has been granted from above, beyond and before any of our efforts; and we have not managed to maintain this image caringly. It may be naive to imagine that beauty will of itself save the world, but there is an inner and innate divine-ness, lasting-ness, and sacred-ness in the beauty of the world, which must at all cost be saved. In *The Possessed*, Dostoevsky himself admitted that the presence of evil sullies the power of beauty.

This is why our destruction can be the beginning of transfiguration, our death the seed of resurrection, our hell the source of healing and wholeness. The damage we have caused and the death we have initiated may be the very means of our only escape from the seeming impasse that we have created. For death and judgment, heaven and hell, are not future events but present realities. We carry them within us, and their consequences are borne outside of us. Death and destruction are not of course part of God's original plan for the world, but this does not also signify that they are therefore opposed to this divine plan. Instead they must be considered as moments of truth. The shadow is the sign of the presence, not the absence of God; just as in the book of Exodus, the cloud that accompanied the covenant people was the image of the glory of God.

There is a need of course to reveal our weakness, to confess our sin. We are required to *mourn the change in the world's rhythm.*[8] We are called to own our shadow, just as Christ never disowns the shadow of his body for which we are responsible. The shadow and the shattering are part of our truth, and comprise our witness to the light and to the healing. For the glory of the world's image is never separated from the agony of the world's currently shattered image. The transfiguration and the crucifixion are not isolated events but constitute the same showing and revelation. The two hills of Tabor and Golgotha are complementary and commensurable. In the shadow of our death and in the face of the world's shattered image, we begin to grow transparent to what really matters. An Orthodox hymn relates the cosmic celebration that results from the cross:

Every breath and all of creation gives glory to you, Lord, because through the cross you have abolished death.[9]

I will leave aside the metaphysical approach to the problem of evil and suffering, and instead consider the positive effects of evil as part and parcel of nature, at least in its *fallen* state. Owing to the freedom that characterizes the dynamic relationship between God and the world, division and destruction are real possibilities. This in no way implies a worldview that is desperately pessimistic, any more than the iconic or sacramental worldview is naively optimistic. Instead, the disharmony and disintegration, while they are very real possibilities, are also indicative and reflective of potential harmony and integration. Thus the cross becomes the dynamic and comprehensive symbol of a world whose image is disfigured, but whose calling is to be transfigured. This of course renders the cross a point of reconciliation and *a rock of scandal* (cf. I Peter 2:9). There can be no philosophical answer to the problem of evil, no satisfactory reason for the mess that we or others have created:

The only answer, the only thing that makes it possible to believe in God at all, is the cross... We do not begin by explaining evil away, justifying God, excusing him for the mess he has made of his creation. We begin by contemplating the story which tells of God taking responsibility for the evil in his world, by entering it himself, taking it upon himself, in all its horror, cruelty and pain...so that by his presence, the situation may be transformed and re-creation begin to happen.[10]

STEP TWO–ASCETIC STRUGGLE

After the step of confession, after the cathartic moment of recognition that things should be different to what they actually are, there follows the step of an ascetic decision to change the situation. *Suffering becomes learning,* as the classical Greek authors declared.[11] The insight that comes from evil and suffering is itself a glimpse into the way of overcoming them. The extreme end becomes the limit that promises a beginning; the darkness reveals signs of the breaking of dawn. The word *evil* needs only to be reversed to reveal the word *live.* For transfiguration does not come at the end of sin and destruction, but must be discovered and enjoyed in their midst. In the final analysis, one learns that there is a kind of *compatibility* between destruction and transfiguration, between death and resurrection. The theologian John Dunne speaks of finding the concrete mean between the extremes of luxury and asceticism:

A man has to find his own way between the extremes, we concluded, going from an ordinary life to a life of thinking, fasting, and waiting as Gotama and Jesus did when they withdrew into the wilderness. Both the ordinary life of self-indulgence and the life of thinking, fasting, and waiting are balanced, we found, by a counterpoint of fantasy, the ordinary life by grim fantasies of decay and death, the life of thinking, fasting, and waiting by wild fantasies of fulfillment. What is revealed to insight in these fantasies is the whole man. The grim fantasies reveal the side of that man that is neglected in luxury; the wild fantasies reveal the side that is neglected in asceticism.[12]

In the shadow of death and in the face of the shattered image, we grow transparent to what really matters. Our predicament of impasse becomes our moment of truth. Our joyful optimism lies in our conviction that there is no place devoid of God. Hell–that is to say, the place where God is not–can only be created as a result of an estrangement between our world and God. If we hold on to *the earth and the fullness thereof* (Psalm 91:1), then everything (even death and destruction) is a ferment of divine life, the air itself (no matter how polluted) is vibrant with the Spirit. Beyond the shattered image, there always lies the reflection of the divine reality that has no end and the re-presentation of the vision of God that knows no darkness. This faith alone can transform evil and pain, while disclosing a loving purpose beyond suffering and isolation. Of course, *sola fides* cannot suffice, for God does not will evil and pain. Yet faithfulness to the earth is never a sign of depression but always an expression of hope.

No wonder, then, it was to Job, in his deepest anguish and sorrow, that God described the birth of creation in this way:

When the morning stars sang together, and all the children of God shouted for joy (38:7).

And in *The Brothers Karamazov*, Alyosha runs out into the darkness of the night and kisses the earth, vowing to love it forever. Dostoevsky writes:

He (Alyosha) had fallen on the earth a weak boy, but he rose up a resolute fighter, and he knew and felt it suddenly at the very moment of his ecstasy.[13]

Repentance is closely related both in theory and practice to the recognition that the world is beautiful. It is a painful return to the start, a costly experience of standing at the beginning of all time, seeing and repeatedly saying with God that everything is *good...very good* (cf. Gen. 1:4,10,12,17,21,25,31). Yet this vision of the goodness of creation comes only after a truthful vision of the evil and suffering in the world:

The thought that it is good, that it is very good, arises to contrast with a previous thought that it is not good, that it is evil. The thinker here stands, it seems, at the end of a long process in which his consciousness has been expanding from a simple awareness and concern about the here and now to an awareness and concern about his life as a whole with its past and future, and beyond that to an awareness and concern about time and the course of human events. In the process he has seen the evil and suffering there is in human life and in the course of human events, but in the end he is able to return deliberately to his starting point, the immediate, to

*become as a child again and to see things with the eyes
of a child. The return to the immediate level of awareness
with its childlike vision of reality is thus a return at once
to the beginning of life and to the beginning of time.*[14]

STEP THREE–THE INITIATIVE OF DIVINE GRACE

If the rhythm of nature is repentance, its pattern is
patience. Step three is in actual fact the first step. It is not
necessarily *our* first step, but it is certainly the initiative
in the process of transfiguration. The essence of
Orthodox spirituality is that, beyond and before all is said
and done, the divine word and act have the first and the
final say. Beyond the innate beauty of this world, we
must *lift up our eyes to the hills from where our help will
come* (Psalm 120:1). The truth of the matter is that the
Holy Spirit in the heavens is the same as that dwelling in
the ground and on the hills. The whole of human history
is related to the story of creation; anthropology is
subjected to geology, while both are the subject matter of
theology. We are required to walk on this earth in
tenderness (cf. Micah 6:8), compassion, and awe; or at
least with the same sense of insecurity and lack of
audacity as when Peter stepped on the waters to Christ
(Matt. 14:27f.).

We must, therefore, desire to see the transfiguration of
the world in terms of bringing ourselves and the whole
world into a deeper perspective (that of the grace of
God), giving it new light and bringing it into a larger
context (which includes the suffering and abuse of

nature) within which it gains new meaning. This process does not bypass the world (= escapism), but fills it with relevance (= encounter). If we do not desire this form of transfiguration, then we do not deserve it. If we do not love the earth this much, then we have good reason to fear it. The infinite yearning for divine grace should never be denied, if we are ever to see the eternal flame that is in all things. *The Lord delivers us, if we delight in him* (cf.Psalm 22:8).

Only when we understand, and take the standpoint of those who are humbled, oppressed, or discriminated, does the *blessedness* about which Christ preached in the Sermon on the Mount become reality for all. When we identify with the lowly and the earthly, then we are all *raised* to heaven (cf. Luke 14:11). When we assume our personal responsibility for the brokenness of the world around us, then we become *the salt of the earth* (Matt. 5:13). To quote another chant of the Orthodox liturgy:

Through the flow of [our] tears, the sterility of the desert is made to bear fruit.[15]

To show compassion to a victim of abuse; to heal a broken heart; to weep helplessly for the dying; to behold a differently-abled child caressing a pet; to thirst truly for life; to undergo the experience of breakdown; to wander in loneliness, and sense the horror of emptiness–this is to discern the loving presence of God in the world. In fact, more than this, it is to feel the peace of God and to see a piece of God in the very turbulence and brokenness of this world. It is to be reconciled, one and all, with both heaven and earth. It is to *go placidly amid the noise and haste (Desiderata).* It is to perceive the undistorted image through and beyond the shattered image.

Discerning the Face of God

The face of the earth reveals a celebration of Easter unleashed.[1] However, as we have seen, Easter presupposes death as well as life, both decay and growth. We need, therefore, to be more prepared to learn from the world, to hear the sounds of the earth, to recognize the Creator in the face of creation. For the freshness of a landscape, the callousness of the desert, and the wetness of the rainforest alike can serve as memories of mysteries and symbols of sacraments. The sacramental character of creation defies all sacrilege on our part, reminding us at all times that the world embodies the divine.

This is the inner face of the world, the real theophany of the earth, the very *sacredness* even of the *profane*. Creation may now be viewed, beyond its gravity and density, as an image of the kingdom of heaven. Indeed, the earth must be seen as a part of heaven. And our relationship with the divine determines our relationship with God. Humanity, we now know, is less than humanity without [the rest of] creation.

It is as though the face of the earth were like the image of God–seen and yet also unseen. And it is as though the face of the world were like a human face–sketched but not completed. Ugliness and destruction only and ultimately confirm the promise of beauty and integration. The deformation of the earth's countenance calls for an involvement in the re-construction of the world's authentic vision and goal. The devastation of the rain forests prophesies the exodus from slavery to liberation, just as the barrenness of Sinai was a sign for the desert people of God. It is this very optimism that characterizes creation itself which lies, according to Paul's epistle to the Romans, *in hope* that *it will be set free from its bondage to decay and obtain the glorious liberty of the children of God* (Rom. 8:20-21).

The struggle is not, as Martin Heidegger believed, between the spiritual and material worlds, but between the desire for gain and the inability or refusal to see the sacredness of the face of the earth. Desacralization must be the first step leading towards trans-figuration; division must lead us back to the reconciliation of all; consumerism demands a corresponding asceticism.

There must in the end–and in the *now* of the *End*–be a sense of *at homeness* with creation. The term *ecology* is itself a synthesis of two Greek words *oikos* (meaning home) and *logos* (meaning reason or purpose). The agenda, so to speak, of ecology is the management of our household, the ordering of our world (which is the literal meaning of the Greek word *cosmos*). The earth is not simply our common homeland; it is our only homeland, and the one thing we *possess* in common. Here, then, at-home-ness merges with at-one-ment with both God and world, revealing at once the twofold aspect of human nature.

Perhaps one of the most powerful and lasting examples that we have of the connections between the earth as homeland and the household is the ancient story of Homer's *Odyssey*.[2] After an absence of twenty years, after losing each and every one of his warriors, and after weeping for his exile, Odysseus is finally approaching his homeland Ithaca. Many writers and poets throughout the centuries have developed and variously interpreted the Odysseus theme. In his poem *Ulysses,* the Englishman Alfred Tennyson (1809-1892) describes an Odysseus who snatches knowledge by possession and domination of the world. But the Odysseus of the Greek poet K.P. Kavafy (1863-1933), in his poem *Ithaka,* gains wisdom by learning through experiences from the world:

Hope your road is a long one. May there be many summer mornings when with what pleasure, what joy, you enter harbors you're seeing for the first time;...and may you visit many...cities to learn and go on learning...

Keep Ithaka always in your mind. Arriving there is what you're destined for. But don't hurry the journey at all. Better if it lasts for years, so you're old by the time you reach the island, wealthy with all you've gained on the way, not expecting Ithaka to make you rich.

Ithaka gave you the marvelous journey. Without her you wouldn't have set out. She has nothing left to give you now. And if you find her poor, Ithaka won't have fooled you. Wise as you will have become, so full of experience, you'll have understood by then what these Ithakas mean.

The English poet is surely influenced by the power of the British Empire; his hero endeavors to impose an order upon the world. In contrast, Kavafy's Odysseus is more humble: he respects the order of the kingdom of this world. Indeed, the suitors of Penelope in the Homeric epic do not honor the household order; whereas, the mere return of Odysseus becomes a recognition and restoration of order. While a house in order is not the final measure of order, where there is a rift in one part, there is a rift in the whole.

It is a question, then, of becoming free of cultural and nationalistic biases, of disciplining ourselves to become disciples of the earth, of being humbled to such a level–to ground level–in order to revere its natural dignity. The calling and challenge is for passionate yearning, not simply passive contemplation, in order to speak and understand the language *(logos)* of creation. It is to form a relationship of intimacy, admiration, and responsiveness. The author of *The Little Prince* puts it this way:

If someone loves a flower, of which just one single blossom grows in all the millions and millions of stars, it is enough to make him happy just to look at the stars.[4]

This presupposes openness and readiness to imbue, and not so much to impose; it requires prayer in order to evoke the spiritual dimensions of creation. For prayer is far removed from any morbid introspection, comprising instead a yearning for the God *who is everywhere present*

and fills all things...the giver of life.[5] Thus the whole
world is seen as inclined in prayer, almost
contemptuously declaring the presence of God. In the
fourth century, Basil of Caesarea in Asia Minor (329-
379) commented on the book of Genesis in the Hebrew
Scriptures:

In the beginning God created a wonderful order...a most
desirable beauty... You are now able to conceive the
invisible through what is visible in the world...so that the
earth, the air, the skies, the rains, the night and the
day–in fact everything that you can see–may be traces of
the Creator... I want the created order to penetrate you
with so much admiration that everywhere, wherever you
may be, the least plant may bring to you the clear
remembrance of the Creator.[6]

Every single thing on the face of the earth tells of the
love of the Creator: it speaks aloud of the unity of God
and of the at-one-ment between heaven and earth. That
is, if it is allowed, if it is heard... Indeed, there is a very
vital sense in which everything in this world not only
reveals but even fulfills the kingdom of God. For God
is still at work on creation; and God invites our
contribution for the completion of this sacred task:

It is certainly true that God is working even now on the
world, like a painter on his picture... As things are, it is
necessary for humanity to collaborate in bringing into
the world beings in the likeness of God, because the
world is already in existence, or rather it is being
created.[7]

This earth is not simply a reflection but a perfection of heaven. The concluding prayers of the Orthodox liturgy refer to the act of Eucharist *as the fulfillment of the heavenly world.* The earthly liturgy is more than concelebration in the worship of the heavenly realm. This world, in spite of its shattered image, remains a completion of the heavenly kingdom. For, just as we are incomplete without the rest of animal and material creation, so too the kingdom of God remains incomplete without the world around us. How can we ever be thankful enough for this?

NOTES

CHAPTER ONE: Introduction

1. Charles Birch calls this the *"atomistic"* world-view that in turn led to the *"mechanistic"* world-view. See his remarkable work *On Purpose* (N.S.W. Univ. Press, 1990), especially chapter 3. Several works were helpful in the preparation of this book, and I need to mention here particularly the authors of the Christian classics, known as the Church Fathers. Paulos Gregorios raised some of these issues two decades ago within ecumenical circles in his book *The Human Presence: An Orthodox View of Nature* (World Council of Churches: Geneva, 1978), esp. chapters8 and 9 [pp. 90-103]. However I am indebted at a personal level to the late Philip Sherrard, not least for his *Human Image*: *World Image* (Golgonooza Press: Ipswich, 1992) *The Sacred in Life and Art* (Golgonooza Press: Ipswich, 1990) and *The Rape of Man and Nature* (Golgonooza Press: Ipswich, 1987).

2. S. McDonagh, *To Care for the Earth* (Chapman: 1986) pp. 8 and 5. This book is an important Christian response to the environmental crisis. Cf. also Bishop Kallistos (Ware), *Through the Creation to the Creator* (London, 1997).

3. This broader conception of sin from the purely anthropological or, at best, sociological to the cosmological level has been developed by Metropolitan John (Zizioulas) of Pergamon. Cf., for example, his article *"Ecological Asceticism: a cultural revolution,"* in *Our Planet* VII, 6 (Nairobi, 1995) pp. 7-8, where the author proposes *"a drastic revision of the concept of sin."*

4. Cf. *Ambigua* 253 PG 91: 1385 BC. References to works of the Church Fathers are, unless otherwise specified, from the classic collection by J.-P. Migne (*Patrologia Graeca* [cited as PG]), which appeared (1856-67) in 161 volumes.

5. *On Psalm 99*, 3 PL 37: 1271.

6. Cf. phrases to this effect in his *Mystagogy* 2 PG 91: 669. Indeed, many of the early Christian liturgies contain thanksgivings for the beauty and goodness of the world. These liturgical texts are *"not cosmogonies but confessions of faith that Christ has conquered and the world is good."* See George Every, *Basic Liturgy* (Faith Press: London, 1961) p. 7. In recent years, not only has the Ecumenical Patriarchate officially declared September 1, being the first day of the ecclesiastical calendar, as a day dedicated in the Orthodox Church to liturgical prayers for the protection of the environment (this was first instituted in 1989: cf. *Orthodoxy and the Ecological Crisis*, Istanbul 1990), but even special services for the environment have been composed, for example by Metropolitan Nikodemos of Patras: cf. *Ekklesia* 67 (1990) pp. 459-62,500-1, and 532-5. The official service for the Ecumenical Patriarchate has been written by the late hymnographer, Monk Gerasimos of Mt. Athos (1991), and translated into English by Archim. Ephrem (Lash). Many of the Orthodox statements on and responses to the environmental crisis may be found in A. Belopopsky and D. Oikonomou (eds.), *Orthodoxy and Ecology: Resource Book* (Syndesmos: Bialystok Poland, 1996).

7. The title of a recent book by L. Boff reflects this notion: *Ecology. The Cry of the Earth and the Cry of the Poor* (Orbis: 1996).

8. *Standing on Earth: Selected Essays* (Golgonooza Press: 1991) pp. 48-49.

9. Cf. *On First Principles* II, i, 2-3 PG 11:183. The cosmology of Origen will be examined in chapter 4.

10. M. Scott Peck, *A World Waiting to be Born* (Bantam Books: NY, 1993) p. 46.

11. *Homily* 48 in his *Mystic Treatises* (Wiesbaden, 1986) p. 30.

12. F. Dostoevsky, The *Brothers Karamazov* (Penguin: 1982) p. 375.

13. See Gregory Nazianzus, *Oration* 28, 23-5 PG 36: 57-60. Cf. also Cyril of Jerusalem, *Catechesis* IX, 13 PG 33: 652.

14. See Gregory Nazianzus, *Oration* 28, 25 PG 36: 60. Cf. also, for example, Gregory of Nyssa, *Against Eunomius* 12 PG 45:932. For a contemporary emphasis on the significance of this all-embracing love, see C. Birch, *Regaining Compassion for Humanity and Nature* (NSW Univ.Press: 1993), esp. ch.2.

15. From the Funeral Service in the Orthodox Church.

16. Theodoret of Cyrus, *The Cure of Pagan Diseases* IV, 60f (in *Sources Chrétiennes* [hereafter SC], Paris, vol. 57, p. 221).

17. See his *My Life in Christ* (Jordanville, NY, 1977 [repr.]) p. 143.

CHAPTER TWO: The Church and the World

1. The doctrine of creation *"ex nihilo"* is usually seen in the Scriptural passages of 11 Maccabees 7:28, Romans 4:17 and Hebrews 11:3. It will be explored further in the following chapter.

2. See A. Schmemann, *For the Life of the World* (St. Vladimir's Press: NY, 1973), esp. chapter 1. I am generally indebted to this fine book for my principal inspiration. I regard his book as radical: that is, as lying at the root of Schmemann's own life and of Orthodox spirituality.

3. See the *Letter to Diognetus* 5-6 PG2: 1173-7. Cf. also *Macarian Homilies* 5, 4; see the translation by G.A. Maloney in *Classics of Western Spirituality* (Paulist Press:1982).

4. Quoted from V. Lossky, *The Mystical Theology of the Eastern Church* (St. Vladimir's Press: NY, 1976) pp. 227-9. See also Isaac of Nineveh, *Homily* 38 (p. 164) where Isaac rejects any *"difference"* between *"immortal life"* and simply *"feeling everything in God"* from this life.

CHAPTER THREE: The World as Sacrament

1. W. Berry, *The Unforeseen Wilderness* (North Point Press: S. Francisco, 1991) pp.16-17. The relevance of the *"sacramental vision"* in the articulation of an *"environmental ethic"* is discussed in M. & K. Himes, *Fullness of Faith: The Public Significance of Theology* (Paulist Press:1993) pp. 104-24.

2. An African Church Father, who was the author of numerous apologetic, theological, and controversial works characterized by a rigorist tendency and concerned with presenting a moralistic picture of the Christian Church.

3. Cf. John Chrysostom, *On Providence* IX, 1 (in SC vol. 79, pp. 145f).

4. See his *On the Creation of Man* 23 PG 44: 209. Cf. also John Chrysostom, *On Providence VII,* 31 (in SC vol. 79, p. 127).

5. Cf. E. Lampert, *The Apocalypse of History* (Faber and Faber: London, 1948) pp. 14 and 164. See A. Schmemann, *For the Life of the World* (St. Vladimir's Press: N.Y., 1973), esp. ch. 2, pp. 23-46. The importance of an eschatological, as well as a cosmological vision of history is underlined by Metropolitan John (Zizioulas) of Pergamon in his article *"The Book of Revelation and the Natural Environment,"* in *Synaxi* 56 (in Greek: Athens, 1996) pp. 13-21; for an English translation, cf. *Creation's Joy* I, 2-3 (Cumberland RI, 1996). Cf. also P. C. Phan, *"Eschatology and Ecology,"* in *The Irish Theological Quarterly* 62, 1 (1996-97) pp. 3-16.

6. *Confessions,*Book III, vi, 11.

7. See N. Nissiotis, *"Nature as Creation,"* in *Synaxi* 14 (in Greek: Athens, 1985) pp. 11-20. For this three-fold vision, readers may consult the work of the late Fr. A. Schmemann: see, for example, his *Church World Mission* (St. Vladimir's Press: N.Y., 1979) p.77 and *Liturgy and Tradition* (SVS: N.Y., 1990) pp.98-99. For biblical references to the creation of the world by God see, for example, Gen. 1-2, Isaiah 66:2, Jer. 10:12, Sirach 15: 14 and 43: 33, Wisdom of Solomon 11:24. Significant work on the understanding of the created world in Scripture has been done by Prof. E. Economou, esp. in his volume *Theological Ecology: Theory and Practice* (in Greek: Athens, 1994).

8. Cf. Niketas Stethatos, *The Spiritual Paradise* 3, in *SC* vol. 8 (pp.64f).

9. *On Providence* VII, 2, in *SC* vol. 79 (pp. 109f).

10. *On Isaiah* V, 4 PG 56: 61.

11. Cf. J. Metz, *Theology of the World* (Burns and Oates/ Herder and Herder: 1969)

12. The word ecstasy is derived from the Greek term *"ekstasis,"* which literally implies movement outside one's own *"proper"* nature.

13. Prayer of the Ninth Hour.

14. R.A. Johnson, *Owning your own Shadow* (Harper: 1991) pp. 108-9.

15. *On the Holy Liturgy*, ch. 78 PG 155: 253.

16. *The Life in Christ*, Book II PG 150: 548.

17. *Against Hermogenes* XXII, 2. Cf. *The Ante-Nicene Fathers*, vol. 3 (Eerdmans:1957) pp. 489-90.

18. See, for example Hermas, *Shepherd*, Book II, Mandate I PG 2:913; Theophilus of Antioch, To *Autolychus* II, 4 PG 6:1052; Irenaeus, *Against Heresies* II,x, 4 PG 7: 736B; Origen, *On First Principles* I, iv [in *The Ante-Nicene Fathers*, vol.4 (Eerdmans:1951) p. 256]; Basil, *Homily on the Hexaemeron* VII, 7 PG 29: 180C; John Chrysostom, *Homily on Genesis* II PG 57: 28.

19. Athanasius, *On the Divine Incarnation*, chs 2-3 (St. Vladimir's Seminary Press: N.Y. 1982) pp.26-28.

20. In this respect, see A. Louth, *The Origins of the Christian Mystical Tradition,* (Clarendon: 1981) ch. 5, pp. 75-97.

21. This latter line is adopted by P. Sherrard in his *Human Image-World Image*, already adumbrated in his earlier *The Greek East and the Latin West* (Cambridge University Press: 1959).

22. The translation is mine, from chapters I, 6 (PG 3 : 596) and XIII, 1-2 (977). See also XIII, 3 (980-981). For the works of Dionysius, cf. *Pseudo-Dionysius: The Complete Works* (in *Classics of Western Spirituality*: Paulist Press, N.Y. 1987).

23. See his *My Life in Christ* (repr. Jordanville NY, 1977) p. 140. Emphasis mine.

24. See chapter 4 below, esp. the discussion on the essence and energies of God.

25. See the following chapter dealing with Plotinus which also explores the transcendence and immanence of God.

26. Cf. Augustine, *On Psalm* 148, 15 PL 37: 1946.

27. Cf. Gregory of Nyssa, *On the Psalms* 3 PG 44: 441 BC. See also Gregory Nazianzus who likens this harmony to a musical instrument (*Oration* 28, 6); John Chrysostom, *On Providence* VII, 11 (SC vol. 79, pp. 115f); and Cyril of Jerusalem, *Catechesis* IX,6 (PG 33: 644).

28. See, for example, Gregory Nazianzus, *Homily* 38, 11 PG 36: 324A. For the interpretation of these *"kingship"* passages in the Church Fathers, cf. Gregory of Nyssa, *On the Creation of Man* 2 (PG 44: 132); Basil of Caesarea, *On Psalm* 44, 12 (PG 29: 413); and Ambrose of Milan, *On the Gospel of Luke* IV, 28 (PL 15: 1620).

29. Cf. Symeon the New Theologian, *Chapter* I, 33 in *Sources Chrétiennes* 51 (Paris 1957) p.58. See also Basil the Great, *Commentary on Proverbs* 3 PG 31: 392 B.

30. *On the Divine Incarnation*, ch. 17 (pp.45-6).

31. See, for example, Cyril of Jerusalem, *Catechesis* XI, 21 PG 33: 717; and John Chrysostom, *On Genesis* V, 4 PG 53: 51f.

32. *Ibid*.

33. Maximus Confessor, *Ambigua* 7 PG 91: 1084 CD.

34. Cf. *Contra Celsum* IV, 16, in *The Ante-Nicene Fathers*, vol. 4, p.503.

35. See Maximus, *Ambigua* PG91:1085. See also columns 1081 and 1329.

36. *Homily* XXXII, 1, in *C.W.S.* (Paulist:1982).

37. Maximus the Confessor, cited in D. Staniloae, *"The Foundation of Christian Responsibility in the World,"* in ed. A.M. Allchin, *The Tradition of Life* (Sobornost Suppl. no. 2: London, 1971) p.68.

38. *Mystagogy* 2 PG 91: 669. Maximus did not invent but was the first to systematize the notion of the Church as the image of the world. Germanus of Constantinople (d.c. 733) writes in similar fashion in the prologue of his work *On the Divine Liturgy:* "The Church is an earthly heaven, in which the heavenly God dwells and moves." See the translation by P. Meyendorff (St. Vladimir's Seminary: N.Y., 1984) pp. 56-7. The concept of the temple as microcosm is also found in other religions: cf. M. Eliade, *Images and Symbols* (N.Y. 1969).

39. See Maximus, *Ambigua* 41. Also see his *Questions to Thalassius* 40 and 63 PG 90: 396f. and 665f.

40. Cf. *Theological Chapters* 67 PG 90: 1108B. See also the fine study on Symeon the New Theologian by A. Kesselopoulos, *Humanity and the Natural Environment* (in Greek: Domos Publications, Athens 1989).

41. See his *De Incarnatione* 20 (pp. 48-9), and *Against the Arians* II, 64 PG 26: 281-4.

42. Paschal Canon, 3rd Ode.

43. Epiphany, *Sticheron* (January6)

44. Prayer, Great Blessing of the Waters (January 6)

45. See his *Ambigua* PG 91: 1057.

46. *On the Resurrection of the Flesh* 8 PL 2: 852.

47. *My Life in Christ* (repr. Jordanville NY, 1977) pp. 141-2.

48. *Oration* XXVI, 13 PG 35: 1245. This radical quality of asceticism is the subject of an article by Metropolitan John Zizioulas, "Ecological Asceticism: a cultural revolution," in Our Planet VII, 6 (Nairobi, 1995) pp. 7-8. On the importance of ascesis, see the article by T.Zissis, "Moderation and Temperance," in the *Annual Theological Review of the Theological School at the University of Thessalonika*, vol. 2, 1992, pp. 29-45. On the monastic dimension, see Fr. Makarios, "The Monk and Nature in the Orthodox Tradition," in *So That God's Creation Might Live* (Ecumenical Patriarchate: Constantinople,1992) pp. 41-8 (and Sr. Theoxeni, *op. cit.*, pp.49-52); see also T. Papayannis and Elissaios Simonopetritis, *Natural Environment and Monasticism: the Preservation of the Byzantine Tradition on Mount Athos* (Goulandri-Horn Institute, in Greek: Athens, 1994). The *"utilitarian expediency"* of our current distortion of the environmental ethic is discussed, from a doctrinal and pastoral perspective, by Ecumenical Patriarch Bartholomew in an article entitled "The Orthodox Faith and the Environment," in *Sourozh* 62 (1995) pp. 19-24. For a more practical application of the ascetic attitude toward the world, cf. E. Theokritoff, "Eucharistic and Ascetic Ethos in Parish Life," in *Creation's Joy* I, 2 (Cumberland RI, 1996) pp. 1, and 5-6.

49. *Hymn* 1, in *Sources Chrétiennes* 156 (Paris, 1969) p.164.

50. See his *Dogmatic Poems* 29 PG 37: 508A

51. *Fragment* 22. See also Xenophanes, *On Nature* 27; Homer, *Hymn* 30 and Aeschylus, *Prometheus Bound* 88.

52. Basil of Caesarea, *On Psalm* 32, 3 PG 29: 329.

53. Cf. the Scriptural parable of the Sower: Matt.13, Mark 4, and Luke 8.

54. Antoine de Saint-Exupéry (Harcourt Brace and Co.: N.Y., 1971) pp. 16-7.

55. 5th edition, Athens, 1971, pp.85-89. The translation is mine. Cf. also John S. Dunne, *The Church of the Poor Devil* (SCM: 1982) pp.132-142.

CHAPTER FOUR: Divine Immanence and Divine Transcendence

1. Cf. E. Osborn, *The Philosophy of Clement of Alexandria* (Cambridge,1957) and S.R.C. Lilla, *Clement of Alexandria* (Oxford 1971). A recent survey of early (mainly Western)

Christian writers and their *"ecologically harmful"* or else *"ecologically responsible"* doctrines may be found in D.Kinsley, *Ecology* and *Religion: Ecological Spirituality in Cross-Cultural Perspective* (Prentice-Hall: Englewood Cliffs,1995), esp. pp.103-24. This book also presents insights from other cultures, religions, and disciplines. Further on the early, particularly the Eastern Patristic tradition in relation to God's presence and activity in the world, see Paulos Gregorios, *The Human Presence: An Orthodox View of Nature* (World Council of Churches: Geneva, 1978), esp. chapters 5 and 6 [pp. 54-81].

2. *Stromateis* II, 2, 5 (3). Cf. the edition by O. Stählin (Berlin,1960).

3. *Stromateis* VII, 10.

4. R. Williams, *The Wound of Knowledge* (DLT:1979) p.37.

5. See H. Crouzel, *Origen* (T & T. Clarke: Edinburgh, 1989). See also J. Daniélou, *Origen* (Sheed and Ward: London, 1955) and H. Chadwick, *Christianity and the Classical Tradition* (Clarendon: Oxford, 1966).

6. Cf. *On Prayer,* ch. 29 PG 11:529 f., and *Commentary on John* I, 7-8 PG 14:32-6. See also *Against Celsus* VI, 68 PG 11:1401.

7. *Commentary on the Song of Songs* III, 12 PG 17:268-9.

8. *On Prayer* ch. 25, 2 PG 11:496-7.

9. See Plotinus, trans. by A Hilary Armstrong in *The Loeb Classical Library* (Cambridge: Harvard Uni. Press 1966). Cf. other works by Prof. Armstrong who was, in this century, a most faithful disciple of Plotinus. In recent times, the *"hierarchical"*structure of the universe is advocated and articulated by the chemist-philosopher Michael Polanyi and by the theologian Thomas Torrance.

10. *On the Divine Names* 4, 12PG 3: 712.

11. Process theology was the school of religious thinking prevalent in America in the early 1970s. Its exponents were disciples of the English mathematician-philosopher A. N. Whitehead, who in his *Process and Reality* (Macmillan:1929) and *Religion in the Making* (Macmillan:1926), maintained that the concept of "process" rather than the concept of "substance" is the key to a proper understanding of the world and of God. Some contemporary process theologians are R. Edwards (*Reason and Religion*, 1972), N. Pittenger (*Process Thought and Christian Faith*, Macmillan:1968) and C. Hartshorne and W. Reese (*Philosophers Speak to God*, 1969).

12. See his work *On Learned Ignorance*, written in 1440. Cf. ed. J. Hopkins (Benning Press:Minneapolis,1981)

13. *Against Pagans* 36f. PG 25: 72.

14. The subtitle of this book is *The Icon*; it was written in 1453.

15. See *Phronema* 5 (St. Andrew's Theological College: Sydney, 1990) pp.15-31, where it is shown how the distinction is apparent already in the Cappadocian Fathers of the fourth century.

16. Cf. translation in P. Sherrard, *The Greek East and the Latin West* (D. Harvey and Co.: Evia, Greece, 1992) p.37-38.

17. *The Greek East and the Latin West* (D. Harvey and Co.: Evia, Greece, 1992) p.36.

CHAPTER FIVE: The Sacredness of Creation

1. Cf. B Ward, *The Sayings of the Desert Fathers* (Mowbrays:1975) and *The Wisdom of the Desert Fathers* (Oxford, 1975). See also N. Russell, *The Lives of the Desert Fathers* (Mowbray:1981). Material from this chapter was prepared for the International Conference on Patristic Studies held in Oxford (1991) and published in *Studia Patristica* XXV (Leuven, 1993).

2. *Life of Anthony* 50PG 26:916A. The Hellenistic romanticism of the desert has been well attested to by Fr. A.-J. Festugière [in *La révélation d' Hermés Trismégiste I* (Paris,1941) pp. 31ff.], but it is the love for the land that is here intimated. We must disabuse ourselves of any *"mystical"* notion of the desert, which is not to be found in the *Sayings of the Desert Fathers.* Such a *"romanticizing"* of the desert will be examined in the next chapter.

3. Cassian 2. For *"remembrance of death,"* see also Arsenius 40, Evagrius 1, Theophilus 5 and Cassian 8.

4. See John the Eunuch 3 and Evagrius of Pontus, *Praktikos* 52 (ed. A. Guillaumont: Paris,1971).

5. Evagrius, ibid. 18 and 97. See also P. Brown, *The Body and Society: Men, Women and Sexual Renunciation in Early Christianity* (Columbia Univ.Press:1988), esp. pp. 213-40.

6. See L. Bouyer, *The Spirituality of the New Testament and the Fathers* (Seabury Press:N.Y., 1982) p.319. Cf. also *Life of Anthony* 14 (864C) and 93 (973AB). For the transfiguration of the body, see also Anthony, *Epistle* 1, in ed. D. Chitty, *The Letters of St. Anthony the Great* (Fairacres:Oxford, 1977) pp.1-5. The biblical source is Deut.39:7.

7. Anthony 10. See also Longinus 1. This understanding is also *"translated"* to the West by John Cassian: cf. for example, *Conférences* XXIV, 5 and VI, 15; cf. *Sources Chrétiennes*, vol. 42 (Cerf:Paris,1955-9).

8. *Saying* 33. Indeed in the ascetic tradition, one who renounces the earthly and yet fails to be satisfied by the heavenly is regarded as most miserable: see the contemporaneous *Macarian Homilies* XLIX, 1 (in trans. A.J. Mason, London and New York, 1921).

9. *Sayings* 5 and Athanasius, *Life of Anthony* 56 (PG 26:952A).

10. B. Ward (ed.), *The Wisdom of the Desert Fathers* (Fairacres: Oxford, 1975) no.11, p3.

11. *Apophthegmata*, Anonymous Supplement, ed. F. Nau, no. 243 (in *Revue de l'Orient Chrétien* 14, 1909, p. 364). See also B. Ward, *Wisdom*, no. 111, p. 34.

12. See Theodoret, *Philotheos Historia*, in *Sources Chrétiennes* 234 (Paris, 1977) p. 268 PG 82:1332C.

13. Anthony 36, Theodore of Pherme 23, Paul 1. Cf. also *Life of Anthony* 50-53 PG 26:917A-920B. See also K. Ware, *"Saints and Beasts,"* in *The Franciscan* V, 4 (1963) pp. 144-152.

14. *Life of Euthymios* XIII, in A.J. Festugière, *Les Moines d'Orient* III, 1 (Paris , 1962) p. 23.

15. *Life of Anthony* 76 (949B).

16. Cf., for example, Letter 575. See D.Chitty, *Barsanuphius and John: Questions and Answers, in Patrologia Orientalis*, vol. XXXI,3 (Paris,1966).

17. *Sayings,* John the Eunuch 5. See also Barsanuphius, *Letter* 569, who speaks of the destruction that may be wrought from the slightest action.

18. Benjamin 4.

19. D. O' Murchu, *Religious Life–A Prophetic Vision* (Ave Maria Press: Notre Dame, 1991) p. 211.

20. Joseph of Panepho 7 and 6, Arsenius 27 and Sisoes 9. See also S. Balatsouka, *Saints and the Natural Environment* (in Greek: Mygdonia Publ.: Thessalonika, 1996).

21. Sisoes 14. The desert is *"the vase"* or vessel through which the entire world is transfigured.

CHAPTER SIX: The Desert is Alive

1. *Apophthegmata* Arsenius 1-2, in ed. B. Ward, *The Sayings of the Desert Fathers* (Mowbrays: London, 1975). This chapter is largely based on material found in G. Ferguson and J. Chryssavgis, *The Desert is Alive: Dimensions of Australian Spirituality* (Joint Board of Christian Education: Melbourne, 1990 [currently out of print]).

2. See the important book by A. Jones, *Soul Making* (Harper and Row: 1985).

3. See W. Berry, *Standing on Earth: Selected Essays* (Golgonooza Press: Ipswich, 1991) p.22. On the notion of wilderness, cf. Vincent Rossi, *"Inspiration: Who Comes out of the Wilderness?,"* in *GreenCross* II, 2 (Wynnewood PA, 1996) pp. 4-6.

4. See Origen, *Comm. in Johan.* 18 PG 14:232C and Chrysostom, *Hom. 17,3 in Ephes.* PG 62:125B.

5. See Palladius, Hist. *Lausiaca* 1 PG 34:1010B. See also Acts 7:58.

6. See Luke 8:29; Evagrius, *Practical Chapters* 48 PG 40:1245B; and John Climacus, *Ladder* 25 PG 88:893A.

7. See Daniel 11:31 and Matthew 24:15.

8. See Clement of Alexandria, *Paedagogus* 2, 10 PG 8:532B; Chrysostom, *Anom.* 10,2 PG 48:532 and Evagrius, *De rerum monachorum* 6 PG 40:1257B.

9. See Clement of Alexandria, *Stromateis* 7, 12 PG 9:505B; Chrysostom,*De compunctione* 2,3 PG 47:144A and Nilus, *Treatise to Eulogius* PG 79:1093Df.

10. See Basil, *Longer Rules* 5,2 PG 31:921.

11. *Historia Monachorum in Aegypto* PL 21:443C and 444C.

12. See *Life of Anthony* 50PG 26:916-7. One also may recall similar stories in the lives of many other saints such as St. Mamas or St. Gerasimos, but especially St. Francis of Assisi and St. Seraphim of Sarov. For these accounts in the life of *St Francis, see S. Francis of Assisi: Writings and Early Biographies*, ed. M.A.Habig (Chicago,1972) pp. 494-5. For the life of St. Seraphim, see V. Zander, *St. Seraphim of Sarov* (St.Vladimir's Press:New York, 1975) p.61f.

13. See Evagrius, *Practical Chapters*, and *Anatolium* 92 PG 40:1249B. Anthony compared a monk outside of the desert to a fish out of water: *Apophthegmata* Anthony 10.

14. Palladius, *Historia Lausiaca* 18 PG 34:1041-4.

15. See *Life of Anthony* 65 (933-6), and *Life of Symeon the Simple* 12 PG 93:1658.

16. *Homily 50, 1 on Matthew* PG 51:513D.

17. See *History of Monks in Egypt* pp. 106 and 149, in ed. N. Russell and B. Ward, *The Lives of the Desert Fathers* (Mowbray-Cistercian: 1980).

18. Archim. Vasileios, *Hymn of Entry* (St. Vladimir's Seminary Press: NY,1984) p. 127f.

19. See *Apophthegmata* Anthony 18, Poemen 58, John Colobos 8.

20. See *Apophthegmata* Poemen 77; Barsanuphius and John, *Letter* 173.

21. See Matthew 23:12; *Apophthegmata* John Colobos 22 and PL 73:966. John S. Dunne records the rabbinical story of a student who asks why there are no longer in our age people able to see the face of God. The Rabbi responds : "Because nowadays no one can stoop so low" (I would add, "to see the face of the earth"). See his *The House of Wisdom* (SCM:1985) p. 20.

22. *Chapters on Prayer* 96 PG 79:1188. See also *Apophthegmata* 7.

23. *Greek Life of Pachomius*, ed. F. Halkin (Brussels, 1932) vol. I, ch.48.

24. See Genesis 33:10 and *Evergetinos*, ed. V. Matthaios (Athens,1957-66).

25. *Apophthegmata* Moses 2.

26. See *Apophthegmata* Poemen 92, 109, and many other similar passages.

27. *Conferences* 15, ch. 7. See also *History of Monks in Egypt* (p.148), and *Apophthegmata* Macarius 32.

28. See Isaac the Syrian, *Mystic Treatises* 23 (Greek text: ed. Spanos, Athens) p.91, and similar passages in Symeon the New Theologian: see his *Discourses*, in *Classics of Western Spirituality* (Paulist Press:New York,1980).

29. *Mystic Treatises* 81 (Amsterdam, 1923) p.306, quoted in C. Yannaras, *The Freedom of Morality* (St. Vladimir's Seminary Press: NY, 1984) p.80.

30. See *Apophthegmata* Arsenius 2. See also Anthony 11.

31. *History of Monks in Egypt*, John of Lycopolis (p.62).

32. Ibid. p.23. See also *Apophthegmata* Arsenius 15: *"One hour's sleep a night is enough for a monk if he is a fighter."*

33. See *Life of Anthony* 4 (845).

34. See *Apophthegmata*, Nau 134, p.135.

35. *Life of Anthony* 14 (864-5).

36. See *History of Monks in Egypt*, Bes (p.66). See also *Apophthegmata* John Colobos 2.

37. *Apophthegmata* Joseph of Panepho 7. See also Joseph of Panepho 6, Arsenius 27 and Sisoes 9.

38. See *Apophthegmata* Pambo 1 and 12, Silouan 12, and especially Sisoes 14.

CHAPTER SEVEN: The World of the Icon

1. *Hymn of Entry* (SVS: New York, 1984) p.81. See also the interesting work of R. Temple, *Icons and the Mystical Origins of Christianity* (Clement Books: UK, 1990) and of Gervase Matthew, *Byzantine Aesthetics* (John Murray: London, 1963.) Also see T. Burchardt, *Sacred Art in East and West* (Perennial: Middlesex, 1967).

2. Cf. Athanasius, *On the Divine Incarnation,* ch. 54 (pp. 92-3).

3. *Saying* 11, in Ward, p.35. Reference to *"all eyes"* is also found in Barsanuphius, *Letters* 120 and 241.

4. *Book* 1, ch. 4 (pp. 15-6).

5. *Ibid.* ch. 16 (pp. 23-5).

6. Formulation of the 7th Ecumenical Council (cf. Mansi, *Concilia* 13:269E).

7. "Preserving God's Creation," in *King's Theological Review* 13, 1(London,1990) p.5. See also the first two parts of this illuminating article in vol. 12, 1-2 (1989) pp.1-5 and 41-45. These articles have, with additional material and editorial changes appeared in a book published in Greek, entitled *The Creation as Eucharist* (AkritasPubl.:Athens,1992).

8. Cf. *Apologetic Sermon 3...on the Holy Icons* PG 93: 1604 AB.

9. *The Sacred*..., Golgonooza Press, Ipswich UK 1990, p.84.

10. From the Resurrection Canon chanted at Easter Matins.

11. *Hymn of Entry* (SVS: New York, 1984) pp. 85-89

12. *Homily* XXXVIII, 11 Pg 36:321-4.

13. *De Ambiguis* 91, See also his *Mystagogia* 7 PG 91:672.

14. *Epistles, Book ii, Letter* 119 PG 79:252B. See also Origen, *Homily on Leviticus* V, 2 PG 12:448-50. Cf. also the fine study by D.S.Wallace- Hadrill, *The Greek Patristic View of Nature* (Manchester Univ. Press: 1968), especially pp. 66- 79

15. Cf. Maximus Confessor, *Gnostic Chapters* I, 66 PG 90: 1108AB. On the priestly character of humanity, see K. Ware, "The Value of the Material Creation," in *Sobornost* VI, 3 (London,1971) pp.154- 165

16. *The Ladder of Divine Ascent*, Step 4, 58 PG 88: 892D–893A.

17. PG 100: 1113A.

18. *Homily* 38, 7 PG 36: 317C. The ascetic dimension to such a world-view is almost taken for granted in the patristic tradition. A positive vision of the world both presupposes and produces the purification of the person. Thus Gregory adds that in our ardent desire for God through matter, we in turn are "purged" and "divinized."

19. For a detailed description of selected icons, including that by Rublev of the Trinity, see P. Evdokimov, *The Art of the Icon: A Theology of Beauty* (OakwoodPubl.: California 1990). Concerning the icon of Rublev, Pavel Florensky once exclaimed: *"There is Rublev's Trinity, therefore there is God."* Cf. V. Bychkov, *The Aesthetic Face of Being* (St. Vladimir's Press: NY, 1993) p.42.

20. *Against Heresies* IV, 21; cf. *The Ante-Nicene Fathers,* vol. 1 (Eerdmans:1950) pp. 492-3.

21. *Sacraments of Life-Life of Sacraments* (Pastoral Press: Wash.D.C., 1987) p.46.

22. *Ibid.* p.68.

23. John Climacus, *Ladder*, Step 27, ii, 26 (PG 88: 1112C).

24. *Hymn* XV, 132-133. As with the concept of *"sophia,"*, so also the notion of *"chora"* may equally be applied to the Virgin Mary (cf. the *Akathistos Hymn*, Stasis I: She "contained [choresasa] the One who contains [chorei] the universe"). The concept of *"Sophia"* is examined in the following chapter. On the relationship between liturgy, iconography, and creation, see the articles in *Orthodoxy and Ecology: Resource Book* (Syndesmos: Bialystok, Poland, 1996) pp. 72-81.

25. See Boff, *op. cit.*, pp.49-51.

26. Gregory Nazianzus, *Letter 101 to Cleidonius* PG 37:181C.

27. In J. Jeremias, *Unknown Sayings of Jesus,* (SPCK:1957), p.95.

28. *Op. cit.*, p.38. Pierre Teilhard de Chardin wrote in similar fashion echoing Maximus Confessor's image of the *"cosmic liturgy."* See Teilhard, *Mass On the World in Hymn of the Universe,* trans. G. Vann (Harper and Row: 1972) p.16: *"Once again the fire has penetrated the earth... the flame has lit up the whole world from within."* In spite of criticism both from religious and scientific perspectives, Teilhard re-expressed in his own poetical and creative language the main tenets of the earlier Christian tradition which are sketched out in this chapter.

29. From the Service of the Sacrament of Baptism in the Orthodox Church.

30. Cf. Dionysius the Areopagite, *Celestial Hierarchy* XV, 7 PG 3:336BC.

CHAPTER EIGHT: Sophia -The Wisdom of God

1. Cf. Frederick C. Copleston, *Russian Religious Philosophy* (Search: Notre Dame, 1988) p. 81. Although Copleston himself holds this view, the relevant chapter in his book is both comprehensive and clear. A fine article by A. Nichols on Bulgakov and sophiology may also be found in *Sobornost* 13,2 (1992) 17-31. Certainly in Russian thought, sophiology is the convergence and culmination of several threads, such as the *"Eternal Feminine"* (V. Solovyev, in his *Lectures on Godmanhood,* 1878), the *"Mother of God"* (P. Florensky, in his *The Pillar and Foundation of Truth,* 1914), together with the notions of *"mother earth"* (F. Dostoevsky, in his *The Brothers Karamazov,* 1879-80) and *"holy nature"* (V. Rozanov, in his *The Family Question in Russia,* 1903). See also G.Fedotov, *The Russian Religious Mind* I (Nordland:Belmont,1975) pp. 386-9.

2. See his *Human Image–World Image*, p.176f.

3. From the doctrinal definition of the Council of Chalcedon (451 CE).

4. *Op. cit.*, p.181.

5. Cf. J. Pain & N. Zernov (eds.), *A Bulgakov Anthology* (SPCK: London, 1976) pp. 144-56.

6. *Ibid.*, p. 153.

7. Cf. John Climacus, *Ladder,* Step 1 PG 88: 633C.

8. J. Pain and N. Zernov, *op. cit.,* p. 156.

9. Cf. J. Breck, *Spirit of Truth* (St. Vladimir's Press: NY, 1991) esp. pp. 79- 98.

10. Quoted in L. Ouspensky, *Theology of the Icon,* vol. II (St. Vladimir's Press: NY, 1992) p. 359. A theological connection between Wisdom (*Sophia*) and Word (*Logos*) was attempted by Solovyev in his *Lectures on Godmanhood,* esp. no. 7. The iconographic tradition is also presented in an article by Fr. J. Meyendorff, "Wisdom–Sophia: contrasting approaches to a complex theme," in *Dumbarton Oaks Papers* 41 (1987) 391-401.

11. L. Zander, in J. Pain & N. Zernov (eds.), *op. cit.,* p. xxiv.

12. S. Bulgakov, The *Icon and its Veneration* (in Russian: Paris, 1937) p. 82.

13. *Ibid.*, p. 83.

14. *The Lamb of God* (in Russian : Paris, 1923) p. 139.

15. *Hymns,* vol. I (ed. *Sources Chrétiennes,* no. 156: Cerf, Paris, 1969) p. 245.

16. Cf. Gregory the Theologian, *Apologetic Oration* II, 73 PG 35:481B.

17. The words belong to Symeon the New Theologian: cf. *The Discourses* (*Classics of Western Spirituality*: Paulist Press, 1980) p. 58.

18. *The Brothers Karamazov,* C. Garnett trans. (Modern Library: NY, n.d.) p.27.

19. See *The Shepherd of Hermas,* Book II, Mandate IV, ii, 2 PG 2:920.
20. Cf. V. Zander, *St. Seraphim of Sarov* (St. Vladimir's Press: NY, 1984) p.32.
21. *The Pillar and Foundation of Truth* (Moscow 1914; repr. Gregg: UK, 1970) p. 326. For an introduction to Florensky's world, see R Slesinski, *Pavel Florensky: A Metaphysics of Love* (St. Vladimir's Press: NY, 1984).
22. Quoted in G. Florovsky, *Ways of Russian Theology*: Part Two (BVA: Belmont, USA 1987) p. 245.

CHAPTER NINE: The Privilege of Despair

1. Wendell Berry, *Sabbaths* (Golgonooza Press: UK, 1992) pp. 13 and 29. The title of this chapter is also the title of a book by Christos Yannaras, which was published in Greek (Grigoris Publ.: Athens, 1973; 2nd ed.: Athens, 1983) and explores an optimistic view of sin.
2. M. Marshall, *"Confrontation and Transfiguration,"* in *Christian 1,2* (1973) p.114
3. *Mystic Treatises* 19, p.73.
4. See Augustine, *Confessions* I, 2-3; see *Nicene and Post-Nicene Fathers*, vol.1 (Eerdmans:1956).
5. *Mystic Treatises* 60, p. 246.
6. See his *Confessions, ibid.*, and Book XII. For the call to repentance, cf. E. Theokritoff in *Orthodoxy and Ecology: Resource Book* (Syndesmos: Bialystok, Poland, 1996) pp. 14-30.
7. Cf. the words of Aleksei Khomiakov, a nineteenth-century Russian theologian, in his work *The Church is One* (SPCK:London,1948) section 9.
8. Words of a Greek poet-philosopher, Georgios Vizyenos (1849-1896).
9. Sunday matins, second tone.
10. Frances Young, *Face to Face* (T & T. Clark : Edinburgh, 1990) pp.74 and 79.
11. Cf. Aeschylus, *Agamemnon* 187 and Homer, *Iliad* XVII, 32. Christian monastic authors also assumed this empirical truth.
12. *The Way of All the Earth* (Notre Dame Press: 1978) p. 61. See the trans. by C. Garnett (The Heritage Press: NY, 1949) p. 280.
14. Cf. John Dunne, *op.cit.* p. 143.
15. Hymn for saintly ascetics, both women and men.

EPILOGUE: Discerning the Face of God

1. For a creative analysis of how people in Australia have tried to become increasingly attentive to the seasonal patterns in the liturgical cycle, see D. Ranson, "Fire and Water," in *Compass* 26 (1992) pp.9-12.
2. See the moving description of the links between marriage and fidelity, and household and earth, in W. Berry, *Standing on Earth* (Golgonooza Press: Ipswich, UK 1991) pp. 49-55.
3. Translation by E. Keeley and P. Sherrard in C. P. Cavafy, *Collected Poems* (Princeton Univ. Press: 1975) pp. 35-6.
4. Antoine de Saint-Exupéry (Harcourt Brace and Co.: N.Y., 1971) p. 24.
5. From an Orthodox prayer to the Holy Spirit.
6. *Homily on Genesis* 1,2; 10 and V, 2. My translation.
7. Methodius of Olympus, *The Banquet of the Ten Virgins II*, 1 (ed. Zeoli, Florence 1952, pp. 47f).

OTHER PUBLICATIONS BY LIGHT & LIFE PUBLISHING

REQUEST A FREE CATALOG

Light & Life Publishing • P.O. Box 26421 • Minneapolis, Minnesota 55426-0421
Web Site: http://www.light-n-life.com • E-Mail: info@light-n-life.com • Phone: (952)-925-3888